"A wonderful piece of writing and meditation teaching. Joan Tollifson moves decisively from self-preoccupation to self-knowing. She takes us with her, in writing that is simple, straightforward, and honest—at times excruciatingly so. The tenacity of certain stubborn forms of conditioning is treated brilliantly. All who practice awareness must sooner or later face and see through such habit-energy.

"This book also provides us with a rare and invaluable record of the teaching of Joan's remarkable teacher, Toni Packer. Joan shows us how she learns and tests these guidelines in the fire of her own life. It documents one person's courageous commitment to self discovery—to 'come-what-may' seeing. I was very moved.

"I recommend this book to Zen, Vipassana, and nontraditional practitioners of mindfulness meditation. When the book ends, Joan Tollifson is in a strong and hard-earned position to take herself and all of us even deeper into the world of mind. She has the rest of her life to do that."

LARRY ROSENBERG, Guiding Teacher,
Cambridge Insight Meditation Center and
Insight Meditation Society

Bare Bones Meditation

Waking Up from the Story of My Life

Joan Tollifson

Bell Tower
New York

Portions of this work were originally published in
Inquiring Mind (Fall 1992) and in
The Inner Directions Journal (Summer 1995).

Grateful acknowledgment is made to the following for permission to
reprint previously published material:
Copper Beech Press: The epigraph "Inside this new love, die" by Jelaluddin
Rumi from *These Branching Moments*. Copyright © 1988 by Coleman Barks
and John Moyne. Used by permission of Copper Beech Press.
Maypop Books: Quote on p. 218 from *One-Handed Basket Weaving* by
Jelaluddin Rumi. Copyright © 1991 by Coleman Barks. Used by
permission of Maypop Books, Athens, Ga.

Published by Bell Tower, an imprint of Harmony Books,
a division of Crown Publishers, Inc.,
201 East 50th Street, New York, New York 10022.
Member of the Crown Publishing Group.

Random House, Inc.
New York, Toronto, London, Sydney, Auckland

http//:www.randomhouse.com
Harmony, Bell Tower, and colophon are trademarks of
Crown Publishers, Inc.

Printed in the United States of America
Design by Linda Kocur

Library of Congress Cataloging-in-Publication Data
is available upon request.

ISBN 0-517-88792-4
10 9 8 7 6 5 4 3 2 1

First Edition

Prologue

Meditation has no repetition at all—
it is moment to moment.

VIMALA THAKAR

This book is about meditation in the context of an actual life. It is based on journals I kept while living and working at Springwater Center, a nontraditional meditation retreat center in rural New York, founded by Toni Packer, an unusually clear-sighted woman who is now almost seventy years old. Toni does not call herself a teacher because she sees conceptual imagery like "teacher" and "student" as obscuring the truth.

As I see it, meditation is not merely a quest for personal peace of mind or self-improvement. It involves an exploration of the roots of our present global suffering and the discovery of an alternative way of living. Meditation is seeing the nature of thought, how thought constantly creates images about ourselves and others, how we impose a conceptual grid on reality and then mistake the map for the territory itself. Most of the time we aren't even aware that thought is taking place. Meditation is realizing, on ever more subtle levels, that it is. When conceptualization is seen for the imaginary abstraction that it is, something changes.

Meditation is listening. Listening to everything. To the world, to nature, to the body, the mind, the heart, the rain, the traffic, the wind, the thoughts, the silence before sound. It is about questioning our frantic efforts to do something and become somebody, and allowing ourselves to simply be. It is a process of opening and quieting down, of coming upon an immediacy of being that cannot be known or captured by thought, and in which there is no sense of separation or limitation. Meditation is moment-to-moment presence that excludes nothing and sticks to nothing.

The meditation approach that this book describes is not dependent upon a method or a program. It questions any attempt by the mind to construct such a program or goal. It relies on no techniques, special practices, costumes, or body positions. It is utterly simple and available to everyone at every moment. It is that which we are, when all that we *think* we are is not in the way.

Meditation is a powerful antidote to our purposeful, growth-oriented, war-mongering, speed-driven, ever-productive consumer civilization, which is rapidly devouring the earth. We retreat in meditation work not from reality, but from our habitual escapes from reality. Meditation is a social and political act. Listening and not-doing are actions far more powerful than most of us have yet begun to realize. But meditation is much more (and much less) than all of this. Meditation is not knowing what meditation is.

This book is essentially a true story, although of course there is no such thing, but it is not intended to be an objective or historical account of Springwater or any other meditation center. It is my story, no one else's. I have made minor changes in chronology, characters, and factual details in a number of instances in order to enhance readability or protect privacy. In many places I have rolled a number of real people into a single composite character for those same reasons, and thus parts of the story have been lightly fictionalized. In particular, the staff at Springwater Center and the residents of Berkeley Zen Center who appear in this book are all composites, loosely based on real people. Names have been changed, except those of public figures, including my teachers (and Toni's husband, Kyle). No character in this book represents any actual person, and the picture I paint of my various meditation teachers is my picture only.

The book was written over an eight-year period, between 1988 and 1995, during which time I was living either in California or in Springwater, New York. It is a kind of spiritual autobiography intended to reveal not some distilled and final truth, but rather the actual messy process of spiritual exploration as it unfolds in the real life of one person, one person who is perhaps not so different from everyone else.

I offer it in that spirit.

JOAN TOLLIFSON
Springwater, New York
September 1995

Acknowledgments

First and foremost, I thank my parents, Dorothy and Wallace, for their wonderful support and encouragement over the years. I extend my deepest gratitude to my teachers—Toni Packer, Charlotte Joko Beck, and Sojun Mel Weitsman—to Toni for her remarkable simplicity and spaciousness; to Joko for her skill in working with emotion/thought, and her indefatigable relish for meeting disappointment and having no hope; to Mel for his wisdom and love; to all three for their integrity, kindness, and steadfast abidance in the ordinary. Thank you from the bottom of my heart to Tanis Walters, Susan Moon, and Lenore Friedman for their faith in this book, their generous encouragement and support of my writing, their astute criticism and invaluable friendship. I am forever grateful to Toinette Lippe at Bell Tower for believing in this book; for her extraordinary care, effort, and skill as an editor; for being such a delightful person to know and work with. I am thankful to all the people of Springwater Center, and those who work with Toni in California. Especially I thank the Springwater staff for all we've lived and worked through together. Many people read the manuscript, or parts of it, and offered useful feedback and encouragement; I am particularly grateful to Michael Rubin, Thaisa Frank, Forest, Maylie Scott, Barbara Gates, Judith Less, Loie Rosenkrantz, Randolph Pope, Chude Allen, Kevin Frank, Nomi and John Stadler, Susan McCallum, Arida Emrys, Judy Smith, Charlotte Painter, Barbara Selfridge, Freida Gordon Dilloo, Melody Ermachild Chavis, Cate Gable, Pat Wells, Blanche Hartman, Connie Batten, and Bernis Berens. For friendship, humor, and hospitality, heartfelt thanks to Paula Kimbro. Thank you to Marcia Kelly, Jean Scannell, Josette Mondanaro, Elizabeth Katz, Lin Davis, Deborah Beadle, Joe Rosenstiel, Evelyn J. Kitson, Isha Mayim, Ellen Mack, Mickey Duxbury, Carole Sierpien, Margie Hughes, and Keith Barton; to the Zen centers in California where I have practiced; to the Vedanta Society of Northern California for their retreat in Olema; to Reb Anderson, Maurine Stuart, Jean Klein, Gangaji; and to the many other friends and teachers I have not named who have encouraged and helped me in so many ways. Finally, I want to express my great appreciation for the work of Shunryu Suzuki Roshi and Sri Nisargadatta Maharaj.

Inside this new love, die.
Your way begins on the other side.
Become the sky.
Take an axe to the prison wall.
Escape.
Walk out like someone suddenly born into color.
Do it now.
You're covered with thick cloud.
Slide out the side. Die,
and be quiet. Quietness is the surest sign
that you've died.
Your old life was a frantic running
from silence.

The speechless full moon
comes out now.

RUMI

Bare-Bones Meditation

1

*It's a common belief that something
exists when it's part of a narrative.*

KATHY ACKER

I was born in Chicago in 1948. I was born without a right
hand. It had been amputated in the uterus by a strand of
ruptured amnion. Newborn, I was brought to a room where
there was a large pillow. My father was called out of the
waiting area and taken to this room by the doctor. My father
was left alone in there with me and the large pillow. He
understood finally that he was being given the chance to
smother me. But he didn't do it.

The doctor knocked. "Are you finished yet?"

My father didn't answer. The doctor came in and my
father was still standing there. Together they brought me to
my mother. I don't know what she felt. She has told me that

this was the only time she ever saw my father cry. He wept. And then he went out and got drunk. It was probably the only time he ever got dead drunk.

My aunt Winifred had a psychotic breakdown at the sight of me, and my uncle Harold insisted on always photographing me from the left side. In some of my childhood pictures my right arm is outside the frame or in the next room.

People want babies, and females in general, to be unblemished. I soaked in everyone's responses to my imperfect reality. I was a kind of oxymoron. Sometimes strangers on the street would tell my mother that we were being punished by God.

Cripples were mostly invisible back then. If you saw them at all they were begging on the streets, or they were the Easter Seal poster children inspiring pity and charity, or they were evil villains like Captain Hook. But they certainly weren't anything you'd want to be, not just because of the physical loss or difficulty involved, but because somehow the whole thing was tinged with creepiness. Disability was one of those things you weren't even supposed to talk about.

The central theme of my life was thus in place early: I was different, asymmetrical, imperfect, special. I was born without the hand that signifies purposeful doing. My life was about unraveling rather than producing, subtracting rather than accumulating. When I was very small and first heard about death, I dreamed recurrently about a person whose arm fell off, then the other arm, then each leg, until nothing was left. I was already on my way toward this mysterious disappearance.

I had a boyfriend in the second grade who loved my arm

with the missing hand. He called it my power bomb. "Hit me with your power bomb," he'd whisper, and I'd slug him gently in the stomach, and he'd grin from ear to ear with wild pleasure. In the third grade he proposed to me, perhaps because of my magical arm.

But more often this arm was a source of humiliation. Children would stare and point and ask me about it. Adults would hush them up. I was the last to be chosen by the boys in dancing school, and I felt that I would not qualify as a woman. Women were supposed to be beautiful. They were not supposed to be missing body parts.

My absent hand was a kind of ticket as it turned out. I was given a passport to marginal worlds, to the realms of the dispossessed, to the secret rooms of people's hearts where something is always missing or misshapen. But it was many years before I realized this. In the beginning, I just knew that I stood out like a sore thumb and that nobody was supposed to mention it.

2

My father was a tall, thin, kind man who owned and operated a small printing company with one employee. He was an inventor in his spare time, who left behind him a continuous trail of tiny drawings on matchbook covers. He chain-smoked, and read me bedtime stories. He told me that when we die, we become the trees and the earth and the wind, that there is no real difference between a table and a person, that the light from the stars is billions of years old, and that the sun will eventually explode. "Could happen in the next second, could happen in six billion years," he told me, "but it *will* happen." My father was a loner. He loved to sit in a lawn chair in the backyard, staring into space, doing nothing at all.

My mother was and still is a passionate and fiercely energetic woman. Her lifelong dream is to see the whole world, to taste everything, to know everybody. An ecstatic lover of life, my mother talked aloud to her plants and to the family dog, and they all listened to her. Everything around her flourished. She believes you can accomplish anything if you put your mind to it. "I do not believe in fear," she told me once. It was her idea to have a child.

My parents were deeply in love. I was their only child. I grew up in a beautiful, affluent suburb where everyone except the cleaning ladies was white and Republican. I did not want to be a woman. I wasn't interested in getting married or being a mother or wearing uncomfortable shoes. I was fascinated by religion. My parents were agnostics. I invented rituals and ceremonies in my bedroom, and imagined myself becoming a Trappist monk or a Buddhist. I wondered why people in India were starving to death while those around me lived in such prosperity. I came of age during the Vietnam War and the Civil Rights movement. I heard both Martin Luther King and Malcolm X speak, and was profoundly affected by what they said, by who they were, and how they were living their lives. They became my heroes. I lost my virginity with a black man.

3

I went off to college in New York State in 1966 and fell in love with a woman. I remember the first time I saw her. It was at dinner in the cafeteria that first night.

"I'd give my right arm to know Greek," Miriam announced to everyone at our table full of strangers. She glanced over at me, took in the situation, and added, "Oh . . . I see you know Greek!"

The drinking age in New York was eighteen, and the only thing in town besides the college was a bar. I got drunk for the first time at that bar. I remember how the colors glowed and my body felt smooth and relaxed and anything seemed possible. I could say and do anything. I came home and lay on my bed and had the spins, and then I threw up, and the next night I went back for more. I started drinking heavily, and also smoking grass, taking acid, and exploring the frontiers of consciousness.

It was while my roommate was in Puerto Rico having an abortion that Miriam slept in my room one night, because her roommate was sleeping with some guy. We lay side by side in the dark, not touching each other, just breathing. Or maybe I was holding my breath. I could hear my heart pounding. It was very loud. I wondered if Miriam could hear it too.

"Are you awake?" Miriam whispered.

"Yes."

"Wanna smoke a cigarette?"

"Okay." I fumbled around in the dark, lit a candle, got an ashtray, and lit the cigarette. We sat side by side in the bed, passing it back and forth.

Miriam blew smoke rings. "Let's play a game," she suggested. "We'll try not to drop the ash. We each take one drag, then pass it back to the other. Whoever drops the ash has to tell a truth."

"Any truth?" I asked, as if there were more than one in the air.

5

I watched the column of ash on which my whole life seemed balanced growing longer and longer as it passed from Miriam's fingers to my own, and back again to Miriam. Finally, as Miriam was raising the cigarette to her lips, the ash crumbled and fell.

"Je veux te baiser," she whispered, almost inaudibly. Our faces were only inches apart now in the candlelight. Miriam had a habit of speaking French to torment me, knowing I couldn't understand it. I told her this now, but I was lying. My whole being understood that sentence, even though I didn't know what any of the words in it meant.

I realized that I had to *do* something, that if I hesitated and didn't act, this moment might pass and never come again. My training had not prepared me for such a necessity. Making a move like that was not in a girl's script. What if I reached over to touch Miriam and she screamed with repulsion? What if I had been imagining this whole thing? Then I would be exposed as a Lecherous Crippled Lesbian. Miriam would hate me and I would shrivel up and die of humiliation.

I was terrified. I drew in my breath and slipped my arm around her in the dark and suddenly everything was moving. Miriam drifted down weightlessly on top of me, her tongue in my ear, pulling me over on top of her, our bodies carried on waves of heat. I woke up at dawn deep inside her large, soft body, awestruck and amazed.

We studied together late at night, took long drives, and sat up in all-night diners drinking coffee and writing poetry. She played Bach and Mozart for me on the piano and told me jokes in French and Russian that I couldn't understand. Miriam thought my arm was sexy, like a large penis. I felt bold and desirable for the first time in my life, but it was a fragile ecstasy.

Miriam and I had to go around pretending that we were "just friends." When men made passes at her, I had to pretend that I couldn't care less. I knew that men had a "right" to make passes at her, and that I had no entitlement to be her lover, and therefore no right to complain. We carried on our entire relationship behind locked doors, in rooms shared with other roommates, or in the houses of our parents, always listening for the sound of approaching footsteps. We sat together at the local bar on the weekends and waited for men to ask us to dance. Sometimes we went home with these men, separately.

4

Hundreds of thousands were demonstrating against the Vietnam War in the streets of Washington and New York. Martin Luther King and Robert Kennedy were assassinated, as Malcolm X and President Kennedy had been. Cities went up in flames as blacks rioted in Newark and Detroit. Tanks rolled through the streets of America. The Democratic Convention in Chicago exploded into violence. There were the Days of Rage and the Weathermen started blowing up buildings.

I read Alan Watts and took classes in Eastern religion, studied the Bhagavad Gita and the Tao Te Ching. I sat and meditated with a little Zen group in the basement of the college chapel. I remember the Christmas bombings, the photographs of Vietnamese children burned by napalm. Men coming home from the war slept in my arms and told me stories on drunken nights, terrible stories, in which American soldiers sometimes did grisly things.

I took speed and wrote term papers, read Ionesco and Samuel Beckett, Jean Genet and Antonin Artaud. I drank straight whiskey and smoked Camels. I took acid and watched Nixon on TV, and realized that the men who ran the world were power-hungry killers in gray suits. My friends and I went to demonstrations in Washington, D.C., and some of us got teargassed and clubbed over the head. The police were the enemy. I was an outlaw.

I hated America. I hated school. I hated the whole screwed-up world.

And then Miriam disappeared one day on the back of a motorcycle driven by another woman, a graduate student from NYU. I got very drunk that night, and when I saw them walking out of the coffee shop, I chased them through the trees, shouting at Miriam, calling her a lesbian. It was my final insult.

I hitched to New York City and wandered the gray streets, crying for days. I wondered if I would ever meet another lesbian. I imagined myself alone forever.

America invaded Cambodia. The National Guard shot and killed student antiwar protesters at Kent State and Jackson State.

I discovered the gay bars of New York City. Strange, alienating places where the women wore heavy butch/femme drag and you had to keep buying the high-priced drinks or leave. It was the year of the Stonewall uprising, when a bunch of drag queens fought back against a police raid on one of the men's bars, the official beginning of the Gay Liberation movement. I slept with lots of men and a few women, too, and I would wake up afterward with devastating hangovers and no memories from the night before. I didn't know if I was gay or straight or what I was. I stood outside the first Gay Liberation meeting at the college, afraid to go in.

"Jesus Christ," someone said. "Next thing you know even the quadriplegics will want liberation!"

I shuddered at the thought.

I graduated from college and became a drug dealer. I took lots of acid trips and lived with a rock musician named Ray. He and I drove up to my old college one weekend to sell a pound of dope. Miriam was living in a house off-campus with the motorcyclist. The four of us got drunk and ended up in bed together. Ray and Miriam were going at it together for a long time. Suddenly I was furious. I jumped out of bed and started pulling on my clothes. Miriam came after me and I swung around and said something horrible to her and stormed out of the house.

I went to the bar and started drinking depth charges. A Vietnam vet had taught me about depth charges. You pour a shot of whiskey into a glass of beer, then drink the beer before the whiskey reaches the bottom of the glass. I drank five of them fast and was on my sixth when Ray appeared. I threw my drink in his face, got up, and ran out of the bar. Ray was right behind me, following me into the night.

"You really are a bitch, Joan!" he yelled.

"Fuck you!" I turned and slugged him in the jaw.

He looked momentarily surprised, then slugged me back, hard.

I remember the sound of crickets.

"Where are you going?" he asked after a long pause.

"How do I know where I'm going? I think I'll kill myself," I threatened.

"Don't kill yourself tonight, Joan," he shot back. "You're too drunk. You'll miss."

5

I woke up in a car full of strangers headed for California, where I spent several years living in lesbian bars, drinking alarming amounts of alcohol, and taking every drug imaginable. But alcohol was my demon lover. I was often violent when drunk. I sold drugs, hustled drinks, had odd jobs that never lasted, took money from my parents, collected welfare, panhandled, went hungry occasionally, and sold my blood plasma for pin money. Once I answered an ad in the newspaper for a "female amputee" and did obscene things with my clothes off while a man filmed me in a motel room. My last lover before I sobered up was a prostitute-junkie who had just gotten out of prison. One night after I had been drinking I threw the TV through one window and the radio through another, broke all the furniture, swallowed a handful of pills, crawled down the highway in search of wine, and woke up a few days later in the hospital with stitches in my forehead and an IV dripping into my arm.

6

If you only realized what it takes,
what a person has to go through to reach
the point of disobedience.

JEAN GENET

I sat in Sophie Cardarelli's office at the Community Mental Health Center in San Francisco. It was December 1973. The room was small, the desk covered with stacks of papers. There were political posters on the walls, and some sort of huge sculptured object made from pink feathers was propped in one corner. Sophie was tall and slim, and she wore faded Levi's, cowboy boots, a blue-gray western shirt, and rings on her fingers. Her long black hair cascaded onto her shoulders in waves, her dark eyes were warm. She had a quick wit and an irresistible smile. Sophie was a lesbian doctor who worked with pregnant heroin addicts and gay alcoholics, and I could see her twice a week for free. I was twenty-five years old, a year younger than Sophie. Ironically, it was my lover Romaine, the junkie-prostitute with whom I had been living, who first told me about Sophie. Sophie had been the prison doctor when Romaine was in for prostitution.

"Have you had anything to drink today?" Sophie asked.

"No," I replied. It was true.

"Tell me a little about yourself," she said.

I shifted nervously in my chair and reached in my pocket for a cigarette. There were bloodstains on my shirt.

"I don't allow smoking in my office," Sophie informed me.

"Oh." I put the cigarette back. My fingers trembled. I felt empty-handed. "I guess I'm an alcoholic," I said. "I get drunk every day. I do a lot of drugs, too."

"What drugs?" she asked.

"Everything. You name it, I take it."

She obviously wanted a more specific answer, so I listed them. Reds, acid, cocaine, heroin, hog, speed. Sophie took notes on a yellow legal pad. "Are you shooting up?" she asked.

"Occasionally. Not very often. I don't like it that well."

She motioned for me to go on with my story.

"I've been lovers with Romaine Karsinkowski. We were living together up in Mendocino. We almost killed each other, literally, I mean." I paused to see how Sophie would react to Romaine's name, but her face betrayed nothing. I continued. "I grew up in a suburb near Chicago. Came out in college. I started drinking then. Came west after I graduated, sort of accidentally. Been in the bars ever since. I have blackout drunks most every day now. And I have these rages. I smashed up our entire house the other night. I think about killing myself. I swallowed a lot of pills that night but it didn't kill me. I just hallucinated a lot. This morning I woke up in the hospital. I decided it was time to sober up."

Sophie lifted an eyebrow. "How did you end up in the hospital?"

"I don't remember exactly. We came down to the city, we were in the bar drinking, and there was a big fight. I got thrown out, and I was running, and I fell and smashed my head open. I don't remember much."

I touched the white gauze bandage on my forehead with my fingertip and Sophie nodded and wrote a few more notes, and then she looked me in the eye.

"How did you lose your arm?" she asked.

"I was born without it." I wanted a cigarette. Or a drink.

"How do you feel about having one arm?" Sophie asked me.

"Oh . . . fine," I said.

Sophie looked at me skeptically.

I squirmed in my chair, sweating now. "I mean, I got a part in a porn film just because of it." Sophie suddenly looked very straight and respectable, and I felt like a pervert.

"How do you feel when people look at your arm?" Sophie asked.

"I don't know," I replied. I had no memory of anybody looking at it. I wanted a cigarette.

"It must happen all the time," Sophie insisted.

I couldn't remember.

Sophie glanced down at my arm. I backed into my chair in a cold sweat. Every muscle in my body tightened. "Stop it!" I begged. "You're making me really uncomfortable."

"People must look at your arm a lot," Sophie said. "It's interesting you have no memory of it happening."

I felt drops of sweat running down my sides. People must stare at my arm every day, hundreds of eyes focusing on it, and somewhere inside of me, I must feel this uncomfortable every time. And yet, I had no memory of it ever happening.

"Do it to me," Sophie said.

"Do what to you?"

13

"Look at my arm."

I felt my eyes riveted to Sophie's eyes. I tried to lower them to her arms, but they wouldn't go down there.

"I can't," I said.

"Try saying, 'I won't,' instead of 'I can't.' "

"I won't . . ."

"It's like you want to make sure the show stays up here, above shoulder level." My shirt felt drenched in sweat. My eyes were glued to hers. "You look at your arm," Sophie instructed me.

"I can't."

"I won't," she reminded me gently.

"I won't look at it."

"Go ahead and try it," Sophie encouraged me.

I looked down cautiously. I felt terrified. My eyes met my arm, focused on it, the strange shape of it. Too ugly. And being seen in the act of looking was ugly, too. I looked quickly away. My clothes were stuck to my back. I was desperate for a drink.

"I want you to make a contract with me, Joan," Sophie said, "that you won't drink at all without talking it over with me first."

I thought for a moment, letting the words sink in. "Okay," I said. Suddenly it felt terribly permanent. That meant I couldn't go and get a drink when I left her office.

"What will you do tonight if you don't drink?" she asked.

What *would* I do? Everything I could think of seemed to have drinking as its centerpiece. "I'll write," I said finally.

Sophie put her arm around me as I left. I felt as though no one had touched me like that for a long time, maybe ever, and I wanted to cry.

I saw Sophie once or twice a week for the next year. Her questions were like koans. What do you like most about yourself? How did you feel growing up as a girl? What was it like coming out as a lesbian? How do you feel right now? Sophie would listen to me and slowly I began to listen to myself.

She did a combination of gestalt, transactional analysis, and radical therapy from a feminist perspective. We looked at how I had (unconsciously) written a script for myself as a child, based on the messages I got from my family and the world around me, and how that script wasn't real. I could discard it. We listened to different parts of me and to my dreams.

Disabled People Are Better Off Dead. Cripples Never Cry (We're Pathetic Enough Already). I'll Probably Fail. Smoking Is Sexy. Sentences like these popped out of my head.

I had homework assignments. I had to look at my body in a mirror. I had to record all my dreams. Friends held my arm, and I spent hours contemplating it myself—touching it, looking at it, talking to it, listening to it. My arm began smiling at me, a kind of wistful, bemused smile. My arm was soft and sweet. My arm began to sing.

Sophie didn't believe that alcoholism was a disease or that there was any such thing as an alcoholic for life, who could never drink again without being plunged back into terminal

alcoholism. Alcoholism was a life script, adopted unconsciously, a choice that could come into full consciousness and
be discarded. If the root causes were exposed and healed, one
could drink again and not become a drunk. The person was
empowered, not the substance. Sophie believed that therapy
should be a short-term process, not an ongoing dependency.

Therapy was a process of listening, of deconstructing
scripts, and rewriting my life story, unraveling and debunking
the old version, and then creating a new one. Instead of
being ashamed that I was a lesbian, now my sexual orientation
and my gender became a source of pride. I became a radical
feminist.

Sophie touched my nerves, made me short of breath.
Sophie knew all my secrets, and I knew none of hers.

"How do you feel about our relationship?" she asked me
once.

"I feel like you have all the power," I said.

"I *do* have all the power," she told me. "You gave it to
me. You gave it to me for a purpose, and when you're ready,
you'll take it back. You'll learn all my skills, and you'll be
your own therapist."

I didn't touch a drop of alcohol for many months, and
then I tried drinking again with Sophie's okay. I found I could
have one drink and then stop. Later on, I had a couple of
blackout drunks; however, there was no urge to have a little
hair of the dog the morning after. Staying sober was actually
easy for me, once it happened. I was simply *done* with drinking,
not by any exertion of will or effort; it just lost its allure.
Likewise with drugs, I indulged occasionally after my sobering
up, but in time my desire for them fell away completely. I
wasn't *interested* anymore in being drunk or stoned, and the

imagined *need* to be was gone. That movie was over with, as completely as a dream is finished when you wake up.

"How do you define graduation?" I asked Sophie one afternoon after I'd been seeing her for about a year. Our hour was almost up.

"I thought you'd never ask." She smiled. "When the patient's life makes as much sense to the patient as it does to the therapist. When the patient has assimilated the therapist's skills."

"Do you think I'm ready to graduate?" I asked.

"What do you think?"

"Yes."

She smiled. "I think so too."

I looked down at my shoelaces.

"Was it hard for you to ask me that?" she asked.

"No," I lied.

She sang me two choruses of "Everything's Coming Up Roses."

"I wondered why you waited till the end of the hour," she said.

"Well . . . maybe it was a little hard," I admitted.

"It's hard for me, too," she said.

I glanced at the clock. Our time was up.

She handed me a slip of paper. "It's a number for a group of disabled lesbians I heard about. I thought you might be interested."

I cringed. "Why would I be interested in a group like that?"

17

I left Sophie's office a month later for the last time and joined that group of disabled lesbians. I hadn't wanted to join. I still wanted to avoid other cripples whenever possible. But Sophie kept urging me. So I did. And to my surprise, those crippled dykes were wonderful, strong, funny women who shared so many of what I had always thought were my own private experiences that I was amazed. We had eye-opening, healing conversations. Suddenly disability was a social and political issue, just like being a woman or a lesbian was a political issue.

7

In the spring of 1977, I was outside the San Francisco Federal Building with more than a hundred other disabled demonstrators demanding our civil rights. "We're going inside the building," someone said, and in we went.

"We're not leaving until those civil-rights regulations are signed," a tiny woman in an electric wheelchair announced. Television cameras closed around her. We all cheered loudly.

I turned to the person next to me. He was drooling, and shouting something utterly incoherent. Our eyes met.

"Rr . . . rrrrrrriiiiiiiii . . . gggghtt o . . . ooooooo . . . nnn!" he said to me.

"What?" I asked, praying that I would be able to understand him this time and wondering what the hell I'd do if I couldn't.

"Rrrriiiiii . . ." He pressed the side of his neck and his whole body twisted around in his wheelchair, rose up, and landed again while he made some inchoate sound and then had to pause and gasp for air. I was holding my breath, I noticed. I let it go. "Rrrriiight oonn," he said again.

"Oh . . ." I smiled. "Right on!"

He laughed and nodded his head, then sped off down the hallway in his chair.

Closing time came and the police couldn't figure out what to do with 150 people, most of them in wheelchairs. They did nothing. The workers left and went home and we stayed. The second floor of the Federal Building was ours, and we stayed there for the next thirty days in what became, as far as I know, the longest occupation of a federal building in U.S. history.

We were a diverse group in every respect. We had every imaginable disability, racial group, sexual orientation, political persuasion, age group, and class background in there. Most of us were disabled, but we had a few "AB's" as well, able-bodied sign-language interpreters, attendants, lovers, and friends who came along and stayed. The Black Panther Party was bringing in our food.

I joined the media committee, which was headed up by a stunning quadriplegic named Nancy Fiery, and we set to work writing press releases, fact sheets, and articles, and giving interviews to the press.

Nancy had very short red hair and mischievous green eyes and sped around in an electric wheelchair. She was, I learned, a former Olympic pole-vaulter who had broken her neck in training, and she had been working in the disabled independent-living movement for the last several years. She was tough, funny, smart, and extremely attractive. I had a crush on her from the first moment I saw her in the press room, but she was married. Nancy and I quickly became fast friends. She needed an attendant and I took the part.

We created a miniature society in that building, and in this society being disabled was no big deal. No one considered it a tragedy. No one thought you were inspiring. No one felt sorry for you. No one stared at you. No one was going to tell you that you couldn't do something because of your disability, nor could I use it as any kind of excuse. It was an amazing relief to be seen every day as perfectly normal and ordinary. I never realized how big a factor such discrimination was (in the world around me and inside my own head as well) until it wasn't there anymore. If anything, the more disabled you were, the more status you had. I found myself feeling envious of the quadriplegics because they were more disabled and got to use electric wheelchairs. Walkies, like me, were definitely a notch down in this reversed hierarchy.

The second night we were in there, there was a particularly boisterous wheelchair race going on down one of the long corridors, and Nancy Fiery and the man I'd stood next to that first afternoon—the man with cerebral palsy who drooled—collided and smashed across the finish line simultaneously, his chair tipping dangerously onto two wheels and both of them laughing.

I happened to be sitting down there by the finish line reading *Zen in the Art of Archery,* which I had found in the second-floor women's bathroom, on top of the towel dispenser.

"Joan, this is Stan," Nancy said breathlessly.

He smiled. They were both breathing heavily.

"Stan's a filmmaker," she told me, "and a poet, and an actor. He's joining the media committee."

"Actor?" I said.

"I wwrrrrriiiite mmoonnolllllogggues . . ." He pressed on the side of his neck but nothing came out. I clutched my copy of *Zen in the Art of Archery*. "Aaaand I per . . . forrmmmmmmm themm onnnn ff . . . illllllmmmm . . . ummmmm . . ."

"He made this incredible film," Nancy said. "He was wonderful. You must see it sometime. Maybe we could get it in here, do you think so, Stan?"

"Ummmmmmm . . . maaaaa . . . ybeeeeee."

Nancy sped off and left me there with Stan.

"Whhhaat aaarrr . . . e youuu rrrrrreeee . . . ading?" he asked.

"Reading?" I looked down at my book.

Hours later we were meditating together.

Soon I was doing occasional attendant work for a number of the quads and paras. One morning, in the same room where a full-fledged church service was in progress, I found myself removing, emptying, and reattaching the legbag of a completely naked man, and then getting him dressed while the church service proceeded around us. Funny how all this was no big deal.

In the same way that gay people automatically understand that gender roles are mostly an arbitrary construction, disabled people automatically understand something about the illusory nature of our attachment to the body, and our ideas about what's normal. After a lifetime of avoiding other disabled people, it was a relief and a joy to be completely surrounded by them. I came into my power in some way inside the Federal Building during that month-long occupation for disabled civil rights. For the first time in my life, I felt like a real adult: working at many jobs, writing articles, talking to the press, being responsible and productive.

21

The group continued to insist that we wouldn't leave the building until the civil-rights regulations for the disabled were signed. Smaller demonstrations and occupations sprang up in other cities across the country. We sent a delegation to Washington. Stan and Nancy and I, along with the Black Panthers and a few old-time Trotskyists, were the radical wing of the coalition. We were trying to make connections between the prejudice and injustice that disabled people faced and the overall capitalist system, to create links with other progressive struggles: women, gays, people of color, workers.

The more mainstream members of the coalition favored the single-issue approach, and wanted to portray disabled people as potentially "good, productive citizens" happily participating in the American Dream. This led to intense battles in the media committee and throughout the coalition, and served as my first awakening to the world of political struggle.

There was no question in my mind that all these struggles were connected, and that the whole system needed to be radically restructured from top to bottom. I thought socialism sounded like the obvious solution, a cooperative society intelligently and collectively managed for the good of all people.

People had love affairs in that building. One couple got married. We'd been in there for almost a month when the regulations were finally signed. There was a victory party on the last night. I danced with Nancy Fiery in the hallway for a long time and almost kissed her, but I didn't.

I woke up in the office down the hall with a surge of loneliness at the thought of leaving. We had organized a huge victory rally outside the building that day at which I was to be the MC. We spent the morning cleaning up, packing all our things. And finally, in triumph, we marched out of the building. People were out there cheering. I was dazed, and blinded by the sunlight. I saw Nancy's husband bend over to kiss her and her face fill with delight, and I felt a twinge of envy. Nancy winked at me, and introduced me to Bob, and I felt a little better.

The rally was uplifting, but then suddenly it was all over. Nancy Fiery was getting in her van with Bob, Stan had disappeared, our little community was scattering in all directions and dissolving, and I was standing alone on a downtown street corner in the blinding spring sunlight, realizing I was back in the outside world again and wondering what to do.

8

I found a copy of *Zen Mind, Beginner's Mind* and began reading it. I read it again and again. I phoned the San Francisco Zen Center, and they mailed me a meditation schedule.

But I never went. I got involved in the struggle to save the International Hotel, a residence hotel near Chinatown, which had been sold to developers who were planning to tear it down to make room for a parking lot. The residents were mostly old Filipino men, who would be left homeless if the eviction was carried out. The hotel became a battleground, and thousands of supporters were there to face the hundreds of riot police on horseback who came one night to evict the tenants. I had been sleeping inside the hotel for several nights. I was sitting in one of the hallways on eviction night, linking arms with hundreds of other people, listening for hours as the police moved through the crowd outside the hotel, smashing heads with their riot sticks. When they finally got to us inside, they dragged us out one by one, bouncing some of the organizers down the stairs by their feet, breaking their tailbones.

I knew by then beyond any shadow of a doubt that the United States government was not a democracy dedicated to helping people all over the world, as I had been taught. I was angry, and I wanted to change things. Our nonviolent resistance to injustice had been met with brutality.

I worked at a variety of low-paying odd jobs. I did telephone sales, I ran a small offset printing press, I cleaned houses, I worked at an independent-living center for people with disabilities, I had clerical jobs. I met a woman who was a radical leftist and we became lovers.

From her I learned about the hidden history of the United States: the extermination of the Indians, the still ongoing theft of their lands, the reliance on African slave labor in building America's wealth, the way we had stolen the southwestern United States from Mexico, the colonizing of Puerto Rico and Hawaii, the evil deeds of the FBI and the CIA, the fact that we had political prisoners in this country, the way we supported dictators and death squads in other countries.

I knew what prejudice and discrimination felt like. After all, I was queer, I was crippled, I was female. I had lived through the war in Vietnam. I had heard the horror stories firsthand from soldiers who came home and told me the truth. I had been there when the police evicted people from the International Hotel. I knew change was in order. I learned about people's liberation movements that were fighting for a nonracist, nonsexist society where the wealth and the work would be distributed more equally. I wanted to join that fight. I wanted to be a revolutionary.

Next thing I knew I was in a radical ultraleftist anti-imperialist communist organization. We were a communist society in microcosm. The needs of the whole group prevailed over the needs of any single individual. You were part of a real community that truly cared for its members. You had a purpose in life, a mission. You were saving the world, fighting for the Good Future. As such, you were part of a worldwide community of revolutionaries.

The lifestyle was rigorous and demanding. I worked during the day, then went to political meetings almost every night, did fund-raising work for the organization on weekends, spray-painted revolutionary slogans around town in the middle of the night, and did as much as fifteen hours a week of childcare.

But I began to feel increasingly unsure about revolutionary violence, especially when it involved innocent people (as opposed to combat soldiers, who are supposedly not innocent). Everyone said it was the only way, nothing less was really effective. A real revolution inevitably entailed the use of force. I struggled so hard to believe what I was supposed to that in the end I didn't know anymore what I really thought. I myself was never armed with anything more lethal than a can of spray paint or a bullhorn, but I felt as though I was part of the revolutionary vanguard.

The people I worked with in the radical left were serious, hardworking, highly intelligent, well-educated, intellectually astute, warmhearted, sincere people who cared deeply about the injustices of the world and felt responsible to stop them. They loved their children and each other's children. They were artists and musicians, doctors, lawyers, schoolteachers, gardeners. They were not at all what you might picture when you hear the word *terrorist*. But then, *terrorist* is a very interesting word, who gets called a terrorist and by whom. There's a certain irony in someone like George Bush calling someone else a terrorist.

I saw more and more clearly that despite our good intentions and our understanding about global politics, we in the radical left were running in large part on self-righteous anger, dogmatism, and simplistic, oppositional thinking: Black Hats vs. White Hats. The mechanics of the organization gradually stripped us of our ability to think for ourselves. I saw us becoming the very thing we thought we were fighting against.

Some people I knew were busted and went to prison for life, and then my father died and I realized that life doesn't last forever. I realized that revolution is real, and that I didn't want to end up in prison for politics I no longer believed in. So I gathered my courage and left.

It isn't easy to leave a revolutionary organization. It's a little bit like leaving a cult. I still believed, in some part of myself, that they were the only real solution to the problems of the world, that by leaving them, I had stopped participating in the survival of the earth, that I was a self-serving coward, afraid to turn over the money my father had left me, afraid to die for the cause.

I took a job in a law office working for twelve criminal lawyers. We handled murders, rapes, assaults, divorces, immigration cases. I dealt with the dregs of a racist, classist, sexist society. Our clients were violent criminals, victims of the system, drunk drivers, men who knock over old women and steal their purses to buy heroin, and a smattering of political prisoners left over from the sixties.

One evening after work I went to the pier on the wharf with an old friend of mine, a woman from the South who was a housepainter by day and an artist by night. We knew each other from the bars where we both used to drink. She had sobered up, too.

She carried with her that same small book, *Zen Mind, Beginner's Mind* by Suzuki Roshi, that I had been reading before I got into the left. She told me she had been going to the Saturday-morning lectures at the Zen center. She said she liked the lectures because the monks would spend a long time arranging their robes before they spoke, getting them just so. And then, when they spoke, they would sometimes leave big silences.

That sounded good to me. At thirty-three I had tried alcohol and drugs of every kind, sex of all imaginable varieties, several forms of therapy, and revolution. Here I was at the end of all that, sober, celibate, and unsure of anything. It seemed like a good time to sit down, shut up, and listen.

Big silences sounded good.

9

I started going to evening sittings and Saturday-morning lectures at the San Francisco Zen Center. The first lecture I heard was given by Issan Dorsey, a middle-aged gay man who was going deaf, who had been a female impersonator, a prostitute, and a drug addict before becoming a priest. Soon I was going to the early-morning sittings too. They began at five A.M., when it was still dark outside.

I loved sitting. The zendo, or meditation hall, was a peaceful, unassuming place that smelled of pine incense. Kerosene lamps and candles lit the darkness. The priests, men and women, wore black robes and had shaved heads. It was all very elegant.

I loved the talks. The point of Zen practice is not to become calm, one monk told us, but rather to simply observe and be aware of the disturbance that we are. You don't know what your next problem will be, you don't even know what your next thought will be. True acceptance is not different from total exertion. The sound of the trucks passing in the street should say as much to you as my words. These phrases rested like seeds in my mind.

I went to massage school. I studied Chinese medicine. I took up karate. I learned to break boards with my arm. I learned to fight back and win. I had never imagined that I could do this, never in my wildest dreams. But I discovered it was possible. My arm became a weapon and a tool of healing.

I studied karate with a Chinese man for several years, and later with a beautiful lesbian who was an extraordinary martial artist. In her school, at the end of each class we would all shake hands with everyone in a lineup, and at first I was shaking with my left hand. And then the teacher announced that I was to use my right arm from now on because my arm was a weapon as good as any right hand and should be acknowledged as such. So every night for the three years I was in that school, my arm was warmly clasped, firmly held, and acknowledged as powerful by twenty or thirty women, one after another.

Learning karate was a way to reclaim my power as a disabled woman. Learning to commit myself on a bodily level, to fight and win, which I had never thought possible before, carried over into every aspect of my life and transformed me. I grew stronger every day. I was well on my way to becoming a black belt when I finally left the school, and I knew that I could have been one if I'd stayed. That was a tremendous shift in consciousness for me.

I quit my job in the law office in early 1984 and traveled to Nicaragua because I wanted to see what life was actually like in a country that had experienced a people's revolution. It was a moving six weeks, to be in a place where progressive people are in power, ordinary folks who believe in things like human rights and ecology and peace, as opposed to people like Ronald Reagan, Richard Nixon, and George Bush, who would apparently do anything for money and empire.

I lived with a delightful family in a barrio, and attended a school in Managua where we learned Spanish and were taken around to learn about the new Nicaragua, which the United States was working overtime to destroy. We were taken to visit newspapers, clinics, farming cooperatives, government offices, and wherever else we wanted to go. I was struck by the level of openness, especially in a country that was under military and economic attack at the time.

I thought I'd despise the United States when I returned. I imagined the hatred I'd feel at the Miami airport. But instead, when I saw the sign that said "Welcome to the United States," my eyes filled with tears. I was home. Horrible as it may at times be, this is my home ground. I found a little health-food juice bar in the airport. I sat down. Everything on the menu had an exotic name. A homely middle-aged woman with glasses was behind the counter. "You want a Nectar of the Gods?" she asked me in a thick New Jersey accent. I loved that woman. I wanted to take her into my arms. She made up for all the evil of the United States government.

I moved to Oakland, into a houseful of women friends who were doing Central America solidarity work, which I also got involved in. I started a massage practice. It was terrifying. You aren't supposed to touch people with a deformed body part. But I discovered I could do it, that my arm actually worked well if only I could drop the idea that symmetry was essential, or that my arm was repulsive.

My uncle Harold and I had our most explosive fight ever after I returned from Nicaragua. He told me I had no right to criticize this country and no right to vote even. I was a free-loader, a bum who had wasted my talents. I had no idea what I was talking about, he said, and no authority to speak.

Central America solidarity work was better than the ultraleft by far—more human, less dogmatic—but nevertheless I grew increasingly dissatisfied with political work in general. I found myself questioning many of the root ideas and assumptions, unable to accept them as I had before.

My whole being was pulled toward my Zen practice as if by a magnetic force that I could not explain or control. More and more frequently, I chose to miss meetings and demonstrations in favor of zazen (Zen meditation).

Most of my coworkers in the movement did not understand. To many of them, meditation seemed self-indulgent and apolitical, a petty-bourgeois diversion that channeled people's discontent away from the streets and into their navels.

My thinking mind agreed with them. The ethics of the left were still running in my brain, and I found it hard to justify sitting in silence on a black cushion for seven days while the U.S. government was pouring millions of dollars into overthrowing the people's government in Nicaragua, and the death squads were gunning people down in El Salvador.

But some deeper, more instinctual part of me wanted to sit. Eventually I stopped doing political work, at least in the way we usually understand it. Actually, of course, meditation *is* political work of the deepest kind, but it took me a long time to realize that.

I dreamed that I was in a big political march or parade. I was marching with a contingent of Hare Krishna people in saffron robes beating on tambourines and chanting. We passed by all my comrades from the left, and they were shocked and horrified to see me marching with the spiritual contingent. I felt ashamed, as if I were doing something terrible. But there I was. There was no going back.

10

I started sitting at the Berkeley Zen Center. One day Mel Weitsman, the abbot and teacher, passed me in the garden and said, "We've never talked."

"Talked?" I said.

He told me that it was possible to meet with him, to discuss your Zen practice. So I signed up. Maybe he could tell me what I should do with my life.

The following week, I went in to see him at five o'clock in the morning. He was waiting for me in a tiny candlelit room with an altar. I was breathless. I bowed to him the way I'd been told I was supposed to, and sat down on the cushion opposite him. My heart was pounding, my throat was dry. I felt as though I were meeting God.

"How's it going?" he asked.

I nodded nervously.

"What comes up when you sit zazen?"

"I think about the future a lot," I told him. "I always do. I can't decide what to do with my life."

"Do you have to *do* something with it?"

"Well, I mean, I think about going to acupuncture school . . . or becoming a therapist . . ."

"What are you doing now?" he asked.

"I do massage. But, I mean, that's probably crazy. I'm always worried about what people are thinking when they arrive for the first time and I answer the door! A one-armed masseuse, it sounds like a bad joke."

"If *you* think you can do it, then they'll think so too," Mel said. "I don't see a problem." He smiled. "What else are you doing besides massage?"

"Oh, I'm writing a book. And I study karate. And I do photography. And political work sometimes, although I'm not doing very much of that anymore. I feel kind of scattered. I start things and don't finish them."

"You have to find the thing you really want to do," Mel said, "the thing you enjoy most. The thing you can't not do. And then you have to stick with it. And not give up, no matter what. You have to let go of the paths not taken, and really allow yourself to deeply penetrate the one you've chosen. Otherwise, you're just skimming the surface, window-shopping, always avoiding what's in front of you, imagining there's some way out."

"But how do I know which path to pick?" I asked him.

"It's usually the one that's easiest, most obvious, right in front of you," he said.

Writing or sitting zazen came instantly to mind. "Maybe I should become a therapist," I said aloud. "I keep thinking I need a career. Something substantial."

"You have to make a choice and then commit yourself," Mel said. "You have to burn all your bridges, so you can't go back. Nirvana is seeing one thing through to completion. Otherwise, life just becomes a lot of mental ideas about an imaginary future. You need to come back again and again to your breath, to the day you are *actually* having. Not the day you wish you were having, or the day you think you should be having, or the day you know you could be having somewhere else tomorrow, but this day that you are actually having right now."

"Jesus," I thought. "This can't be it."

"Are you still holding out the hope that you'll get there someday?" Mel asked. "That you'll find your ideal life?"

"I know it's impossible, but I'm still holding out the hope," I admitted.

"Your meditation practice will teach you the impossibility." He smiled. "Some people spend their whole lives looking for it, but never doing it," he said. "What is it?" he asked.

I wondered.

"That's your natural koan," Mel told me later. "What is it? Keep asking that question, all the time. Don't try to answer it. Just keep asking. What is it?"

What is it? Wind, bus, thought, insect, sensation, sound, smell, breath. What is it?

All my life I've been waiting for something to happen.

"When thoughts come, you can invite them in," Mel told

us in one of his lectures, "but don't serve them tea." He smiled. "Zen teaches you how you think," he said. "It's about watching the movie that's going on inside your head, the one you're acting in, and beginning to see it for the first time. Be aware of your physical sensations, your breath, your thoughts. Don't try to change anything. Just see it."

He looked at us and paused for a long time. I heard the raindrops on the roof and the birds singing in the courtyard. I heard car tires on the wet street.

When you just sit there doing nothing, you discover that there is a tremendous amount happening: plans, memories, physical sensations, emotions, impulses, desires, likes and dislikes, fears, fantasies, judgments.

"In Zen," Mel says, "we just watch. Just be aware."

"Enlightenment isn't about getting something," he told us. "With any great Zen master, it's not what they have, it's what they don't have."

I loved the sense of freedom, the relief of finally just sitting down and doing nothing at all. Listening quietly for the first time. Simply being alive. Hearing the rain.

"You are perfect just the way you are," Mel said to me, "but that doesn't mean that there isn't room for improvement. Each moment is perfect, but you don't have to hold on to it."

"I want you to be my teacher," I told him.

"Thank you," he said.

11

I signed up for my first seven-day sesshin. A Zen sesshin is a kind of mind-washing, Mel told me. A whole week of meditation. The days are spent sitting zazen, doing walking meditation, bowing and chanting, working together in silence, eating formal meals in the zendo in an elaborate ceremonial fashion, and having private meetings with the teacher. Aside from these meetings, the ceremonies, and a daily lecture, there is complete silence for the entire week and no eye contact between participants. The schedule is compulsory and rigorous. You *must* sit, and you sit through pain or whatever arises, without moving.

So much communion exists without words or eye contact. I am struck by the intimacy I feel with these people, with the person who sits next to me for seven days.

In sesshin, we sit with our pain and do not move away from it. We sit with our desires and do not move toward them. We eliminate all the outward escapes from our suffering. We really get to know it. What is it? We watch the obsessive loops of our thinking. We eat in silence. Servers bring us food, bow to us, and bring hot water afterward with which we wash our bowls. The smallest tasks become sacred. Washing our eating bowls. Folding our napkins. Form is not sacred, Mel says, but form allows the sacred to emerge.

It gets painful. My legs hurt, my back aches, my feet are cold, my eye itches. I don't move when the pain comes. If I resist the pain, seeing it as something outside of myself that is attacking me, something I want to get away from, then it begins to frighten and overwhelm me. The only way through it is to be very still and open to it.

"It's important to reach the point where you think that you can't continue for another second," Mel says, "and then it's important to continue."

"I'm having a crisis of faith in Zen," I told him at one point. I had cramps and a headache, my back was killing me, and I didn't feel like sitting in a freezing-cold room at 4:30 in the morning trying not to move.

"There is no Zen," Mel replied. "It's what's inside of you. Where's your spirit?"

"I'm in pain," I told him. "This feels like nothing but a crazy macho endurance contest."

"Endurance is everything," he told me. "It's your ability to see things through to completion. We always want to go somewhere else or get something we don't have. We think that if only we move to a new house or find a new job or a new girlfriend, or get enlightened, then we'll finally be happy. But the trouble is, no matter where we go or what we do, we take ourselves along. And that's the real problem. Here in sesshin we face that. We don't move at all. The whole point of sesshin is to have no way out. Because if there's a way out, we take it. This is where the buck stops. This is the last place. Here, we just have to settle in exactly where we are. Because really, this moment is all we ever have."

"I can see the benefits of that kind of practice," I began, "but—"

Mel cut me off. "Benefits, benefits," he repeated with irritation. "No! Just do it! This isn't about benefits. It isn't about getting something or becoming somebody. It's just this. Nothing else!"

I can't imagine living without the idea of getting somewhere, or becoming somebody. I feel as if my mind will crack any second. But somehow I keep going. Days and nights go by. Watching for the thoughts to come up. And then noticing that they have already come and swept me away.

"What about the world situation?" I asked Mel.

"This practice will help us know what to do to save the world," he told me. "We *are* the world."

Mel says that small mind sees the enemy as outside of ourselves and conceives the answer as bigger and bigger guns. Big Mind sees the enemy in myself and myself in the enemy.

I am less and less inclined to locate the enemy "out there" somewhere, and less and less drawn to violent revolution as the best path to liberation. It may well be the only path in many cases (I would not presume to judge the tactics of people in life-threatening situations), but for me, it feels less and less like the way I want to go. It is frightening, after all these years as a leftist, to acknowledge this shift in my consciousness.

"Thank you all for making this great effort," Mel said to us at the end of the sesshin. "It would be very hard to sit a sesshin alone." His ears seemed extraordinarily large. There was a long silence. At last Mel spoke: "Life is one long sesshin from which there is no escape."

12

I moved into the Berkeley Zen Center as a resident finally, and lived there for several months. I had decided to get to the root of the matter. I had this idea that I wanted to spend my life carrying small bundles of firewood, sweeping out rooms, cooking vegetables, chanting sutras, following my breath back to the source. I would get to the silence below the words, make my life itself the work of art. Become weightless. Utterly simple. I could see myself as a priest, my head shaved like Mel's, wearing long black robes and carrying incense. It's a very sensual place, a Zen center. Everything there is a work of art. Every doorknob is polished.

Of course, the schedule was demanding. Getting up every morning at 4:30. I couldn't do that and still be intact for an evening karate class. And my heart was more in karate than Zen. Furthermore, I was the only queer there. I'd look around and see these heterosexuals in black robes looking very serious and chanting in Japanese to the Buddha, and I'd think, What the hell am I doing here? Why are we all pretending to be in medieval Japan?

Everything was spotless. The aesthetic was impeccable. Mel was fastidious about every little detail in a way that began to irritate me no end. I dreamed that there were Latin dancers in the meditation hall. Black women in brightly colored dresses. The Zen priests in their black robes were all singing. Mel carried a huge tambourine, the size of a bicycle tire, and kept time.

"I'm not sure I belong here," I said to Mel at last. "At the Zen center, I mean. Maybe it was a mistake."

"If you're going to live here," he told me, "then your Zen practice has to be your first priority. If it isn't, then go do something else. And make that your practice. We have too many choices in this culture," Mel said. "Too much luxury, too much freedom. Everywhere we go we're presented with opportunities. Buy this . . . try this activity . . . go to this place. Creating desire is a billion-dollar industry. Any one of these things we're tempted with can become a whole way of life. We take up some new activity and then pretty soon we either have to drop it or devote ourselves to it, or else we find ourselves trying to do twenty different things at once, and doing all of them in a superficial way."

I smiled.

"In a certain sense," Mel continued, "limitation is freedom. Then you can let go of all the fantasies, all the possibilities, and just settle into what's actually in front of you. You find that really, the thing itself isn't so important, whether it's this activity or that one. But the settling in and penetrating to the root is very important. That's what sesshin is all about. Right now you're here. Exactly here. Energy needs to focus or else it turns to restlessness and daydreaming. Our suffering is our inability to settle. Suffering is believing there's a way out."

Later he told me, "We're always looking for diamonds in the mud. But actually the mud itself is pretty interesting. That's what Zen practice is about. The mud."

13

I moved out of the Zen center, and lived alone in Oakland. I continued to meditate, mostly on my own. I went back to school and got a graduate degree in creative writing. I dreamed that at the graduation ceremony they gave us right hands instead of diplomas.

I took the basic co-counseling class. The first exercise we were given to do made a strong impression on me. We were paired up with a partner and one person was the speaker and the other was the listener for half an hour, then we switched roles for the second half hour. The listener was supposed to just listen. Nothing else. We were told to notice the urge to intervene, to fix this person, to offer advice, to tell them about the things in our own life that their experiences reminded us of. But instead of acting on these urges, we were told to simply listen. We were to notice our facial expressions and maintain a relaxed, neutral expression, as opposed to having looks of grave concern or sympathy on our faces. I was struck by how healing it is simply to be heard.

Meditation became my primary interest. I sat with Joko Beck, an innovative teacher from San Diego with great passion for her work and a notoriously sharp eye. Joko is probably in her seventies, and she's a down-to-earth, no-frills Zen teacher who stresses understanding the nature of the thought process and experiencing emotion as bodily sensation. As a basic practice, she advises her students to label their thoughts and then return to pure sensation. Joko has you use a full sentence label, beginning with the line "Having a thought that . . ." So you might say, "Having a thought that the person next to me is breathing too loudly," or "Having a thought that Zen is useless." As Joko points out, there's a big difference between: "Bill is a jerk" and "Having a thought that Bill is a jerk." You notice how repetitive your thought patterns are, and it becomes quite comical.

I loved working with Joko, but Toni Packer was coming to town and I had already signed up for my first retreat with her, so I went. I was expecting it to be a Zen sesshin without the trappings, but it wasn't a sesshin at all. It was something entirely new to me.

I remember my first glimpse of Toni: a white-haired woman wearing ordinary, comfortable clothes—sweatpants, maybe—in bright colors. There was an urgency and an immediacy in her talks. She swayed back and forth with her eyes closed, as if dancing, reaching for something unimaginably delicate. She seemed beautiful and sensual to me then, alive and vibrant, intensely interested in what she was doing, inquiring into the mind, and able to talk about meditation in the most straightforward language.

Listening to those talks, it was as if the lights had been turned on, and something became clear to me. I realized that the whole story of "me" is imaginary, that "I" exist as a separate, discrete individual only when I think of myself. Without this thought of me and my story, everything is permeable, spacious, without division. The thought of "me" is so powerfully conditioned, so seemingly real, so socially accepted, that we take it as an unquestioned fact. We exist, in our thoughts, as separate selves by telling stories to ourselves and each other.

The most striking thing was the effortless quality of Toni's work. Something imposed and willful had been deleted. Toni seemed to take a step beyond anything I had encountered before, revealing that the observer-meditator and all of its "practices" are also thought. I began to wonder anew what meditation is. I was surprised to discover how good it felt to drop all the rituals and paraphernalia. It was so quiet, so natural.

I flew immediately to Springwater for a retreat.

14

I challenged a lot of people with my conviction that everything is meaningless and of no value, that everything returns to nothingness. But this was too much, or too little, for the everyday world to conceive. . . . I could only think of this concept of nonusefulness as being of great benefit to the world, and particularly the present world which is moving so rapidly in the opposite direction.

"How about not *doing this?" "How about* not *doing that?"—
that was my way of thinking.*

MASANOBU FUKUOKA, *The One-Straw Revolution*

The plane flew into dark storm clouds that rose up everywhere and engulfed us. We rocked and shuddered on the choppy air. This is weather, I remember thinking—real weather, not the ever-mild, always-pleasant Bay Area. It was July when I went to Springwater the first time. I had the idea of joining the staff and moving there already percolating in the back of my mind. Coming into Rochester by air, I remember seeing the earth below me and being amazed by how green it was. I grew up in this part of the world, but twenty years in California had accustomed me to drier, less verdant land.

I stepped off the plane and a big man named Roger from Springwater was there to greet me. He smelled of motor oil, his face was worn but gentle, and everything about him seemed in slight disarray. Roger carried my suitcases to a blue Dodge van, and drove me to Springwater, which is about an hour away. I liked the flowing green farmland we passed through, and I liked Roger. There was something sincere and trustworthy and endearing about him, and perhaps I already sensed that he was a man who wasn't going to fall for any of my pretensions or flatter my ego; while I found that slightly irritating and unnerving, I also found it appealing.

When we turned finally into the long driveway to the center, I felt nervous and excited. The driveway meandered through the woods and finally emerged in a big, open area. A large, plain wooden building appeared in front of us, built into the hillside.

Roger unloaded my luggage and ushered me inside. We took off our shoes and left them on a shoe rack by the front door. Another man on staff appeared, showed me to my room, and toured me around the building. Felix had curly black hair and a soft voice, and his presence vibrated with quiet. He said nothing extra, and managed to make me feel very much at home and comfortable.

There is a spareness at Springwater that I loved immediately. The building is open and light, with big windows everywhere. It includes bedrooms for staff and guests, a large kitchen, showers and a hot tub, a dining room, an exercise room with a small library, offices, a separate small apartment for Toni and her husband, Kyle, to use when they are in residence, and a large meditation room. People here built this whole place from scratch on a shoestring budget. Many of them learned how to do carpentry and plumbing in the process. Some of the trim work is still unfinished, but for the most part, the building is complete. Roger and Felix have been here from the beginning. They both helped build the place.

The meditation room is a simple, light room with a handsome wooden floor, and large floor-to-ceiling windows overlooking the fields and forests. There are sumptuous green plants, cushions of every size and variety for comfort in sitting, and an ample supply of chairs and balance-chairs. This room, like the rest of the building, feels warm, natural, spacious—uncluttered by objects, trimmings, or ideas.

I walked uphill by myself into a field as the sun was going down that first night, and came to a small pond. I sat down and felt my whole body relax. The air was warm and moist, and smelled of blossoms and grasses. Everything was lush and fragrant. The hillside across the valley turned a deep red. Bats skimmed the surface of the water, swooping in front of me. There were metallic rustlings in the grass, and an almost-deafening cacophony of frogs and insects jingling and croaking. I heard the exquisite song of a bird I had never heard before, and then an owl hooting and a dog answering in the distance. Huge red clouds floated past. I'd never been anywhere so alive.

The land here is beautiful in an unspectacular way. It's not the Grand Canyon or Yosemite. It's much quieter, more subtle. More than two hundred acres of fields, rolling hills, woods, cascading streams, hemlock-lined ravines, farm ponds, tiny miracles. And weather that is stormy and passionate and ever-changing.

Springwater was originally the Genesee Valley Zen Center, but over time the Zen forms, names, and ideas were dropped, and by the time I showed up, it no longer thought of itself as a Zen center in the usual sense of the word. It had gotten much, much plainer. All the trappings of religion have been stripped away. (Perhaps a little too dogmatically at times: "Incense is a drug," Sharon—the only woman on staff— actually said to me.) There are no rituals or ceremonies. Just the bare bones of ordinary life, questioning everything, not knowing where it will end up. Discovering that awareness does not depend on any practices, postures, or traditions, looking at every form of attachment. Nothing to hold on to: no legitimated "way" to follow, no career priesthood to join, nothing.

No formal practice is recommended (following or counting the breath, labeling thoughts, working on koans, visualizations, mantras). When meditating, don't do anything at all, Toni advises. Just listen.

> *No matter what state dawns at this moment, can there be* just that? *Not a movement away, an escape into something that will provide what this state does not provide, or doesn't seem to provide: energy, zest, inspiration, joy, happiness, whatever. Just completely, unconditionally listening to what's there now, is that possible? Without having a judgment about it, a conclusion—that this is bad, that if I don't do something about it that it will be this way forever, that it needs help—wanting to be rid of it. And one hasn't begun to explore it.*
>
> TONI PACKER

Toni is unsentimental and uncompromising in her insight, but at the same time gentle and caring. She is passionate about questioning how the mind works and goes persistently to the root. There is a sobriety in her approach, an austerity that is warmhearted but meticulously unseductive. That which is extraordinary about her, and about Springwater, is so unconnected to pretenses or posturing of any kind, that you could miss it entirely. It is a quality of undefended openness, innocence in the truest sense.

Toni has the courage to put aside all the books, all the

methodologies, and just be with the moment itself, no props or extras, no authorities, no beliefs. She is listening as she talks, looking at what it is she's talking about as if for the first time. She's not speaking out of intellectual knowledge. She loves nature, and her voice emerges from stillness like wind in leaves.

Springwater holds eight one-week silent retreats every year, and a number of shorter retreats. People come from all over the country, and the world, to attend them.

Outside of retreats there is daily work (roughly forty hours a week), but otherwise no schedule to follow. A small resident staff maintains the center and organizes the retreats. Many of them, like Felix and Roger, have been here from the beginning. Right now, all of them except Sharon are men. The average age on staff seems to be around forty. A few guests and long-term volunteers are usually in residence at any given time as well.

There is a feeling of kindness here. The atmosphere is gentle, nonjudgmental, spacious. I don't feel that people are trying to impress me, seduce me, charm me, flatter me, or get something out of me. The place has a non-invasive quality, allowing things to be.

I am impressed by how smoothly everything works, how well organized it all is despite the absence of any kind of heavy-handed hierarchical structure or discipline. But people on staff watch television. I was very disappointed to discover that. I imagined them all meditating, baking bread, walking in the woods. But not watching television. And then, the second night I was here, my bedroom was suddenly filled with rock music. It was coming from the room below mine—Paul's room, one of the men on staff—and it was so loud that the walls in my room vibrated. I was shocked. Horrified. How would I be able to meditate with *this* going on!? Rock music and television were not in my picture of a meditation center. Perhaps I wouldn't want to live here after all.

15

*There is nothing in all the universe
so much like God as silence.*

MEISTER ECKHART

My first retreat at Springwater begins. Complete silence is carefully maintained on these week-long retreats. Eye contact is discouraged so that one can be completely inward and not caught up in constantly making connections or scanning to see how others are responding to you. Any necessary communication is done with pencil and paper. The only exception is that you can meet with Toni once a day if you want to, and every day she gives a talk. I have never been anywhere in my whole life where silence was this resonant and bottomless.

During retreats, you don't have to sit in the sitting room if you prefer not to. You can sit in armchairs or on the sofa in the adjoining rooms, you can lie in bed all day, or sit up at the pond, or walk. Nothing is required. Toni places great emphasis on letting the wisdom of the organism itself unfold.

Toni's talks are meditations in themselves. They require enormous listening-participation. You cannot listen casually.

You have to listen out of silence and inward looking. And the looking is not intellectual; it's a different process.

I feel the constant impulse to write down her words. But just the seeing itself is the thing, she says, not remembering or knowing it. This feels risky, hard to trust. What if I lose some important piece of insight and miss my Big Chance? Big Chance for what? What is it we're trying so hard to get?

What is wanting? We're so busy with wanting something else that we don't take time to find out what this is, right now, right here. Thoughts and ideas are everywhere. "Liberation" is an idea. Something I want. Trying to think our way out of this mess doesn't work. I only get more and more confused and entangled. Don't trust thinking, Toni says.

Hours of churning thoughts and then something opens and there is just the wind, the buzzing of the flies, the rush of thoughts, the floor underfoot, all at once, in wholeness. Everything relaxes, becomes spacious. I really see that there's nothing to get, nowhere to go, no one to get there. There is no "I" anymore, no center. No fear. No time.

But then, so quickly comes the urge to capture this moment of awakening: to possess it, keep it, have it again, have it forever.

"I need to learn to just trust that awareness," I tell Toni.

"What do you mean by trusting?" she asks.

I laugh, seeing that what I mean is counting on it to get an imagined "me" to where I want to go. It is a departure into thought and image, into the idea of time, and it brings pleasant feelings and relief from the thought that "awareness is not enough to make me happy," which brings unpleasant feelings.

"What can you trust?" Toni asks. "You don't know. Don't trust anything. Watch how thought comes in so quickly."

Toni asks me what is the "I" that is observing (and trying to improve) "me"?

It is a thought! A picture of "me" watching "me." The observer is nothing more than a construct of memory and conditioning, a little dictator who lives in my head and shouts commands at some imaginary self she is trying to get in shape, commands like "Come back to the moment!" "Listen to the birds!" "Pay attention to the breath!" "Stop fantasizing!"

I am trying so hard. My whole being is utterly tensed from head to toe with *effort*. Trying to do it right. At one point, I think that Toni is walking behind me during a walking period, and spend the entire period watching myself trying to "walk perfectly," then trying to "just relax" and "not try," trying so hard either way to "do it right" that it's a wonder I can even walk, then realizing at the end that it wasn't even her walking behind me. All of it just images in my head, but they run my whole mind-body.

Just to see them is enough. Seeing the performance, the ideas, the conflicting commands, the effort not to perform, the desire to be someone else, someone who isn't trapped in such ridiculous behavior. Seeing the idea of "me" in the middle of all of this. Just seeing.

The magenta cushions in the meeting room, the extraordinary bouquet of flowers, the mist outside the window, our words. It can't be grasped or preserved. This text is something else entirely. This text, like all texts, is a fiction. An event in itself. A kind of birdsong. Not unlike the buzzing of the flies or the smell of the flowers.

Walking in the afternoon, I pass Toni in a field of wildflowers and light. She passes me like a great gust of strong wind.

There was a storm last night, and the wind was like an ocean, roaring waves rolling over the fields, whipping the trees this way and that. There was thunder and lightning. And rain, cooling the earth.

The constant printout of thoughts: commands and countercommands—*Try, Don't Try*—planning the future, imagining all the terrible or pleasant things that could happen to me, or else endlessly running through memory replays like someone watching and rewatching the reruns of an old television program, giving speeches in my head, endless noise and chattering. Even when I wake up to the thoughts, I'm often unable or unwilling to let them go. They're as compelling as any other addiction, maybe much more so. I'm addicted to myself. Why is it so scary, so hard to let these thought-loops go? I feel frustrated and close to despair.

Wanting something and going for it, we condition the mind, Toni says. Here we just watch. Watching the nature of wanting itself. Burning pain in my shoulder and neck, anger, frustration, irritation, exhaustion. Everyone makes me angry. Everything irritates me. There is a gray cloud around my mind. No clarity. I don't want to be here for another minute in this painful, unmoving posture, in this noisy silence that won't shut up, in this body or this mind. What is all this about "no self," I think to myself. What about my history, my suffering, my progress—aren't these me? I feel the urge to bite my fingers.

Swarms of deerflies buzz and snarl around my ears and tangle in my hair. Mosquitoes land on my neck. Clouds hang in the sky. Thunder crackles in the distance. Sweat drips down my arms.

What is awareness? I'm not even sure I know anymore.

Is there anything at all outside of thought and image? Once we know language, once we learn to see the accepted boundaries that divide the chair from the table and the table from us, once we start to think in concepts, once we become conditioned, is there really any way out of it? A moment of direct sensation, listening openly—and then instantly thought is there labeling, evaluating, separating, comparing, making something out of it—and the listening is gone. Maybe it was never there at all. Are we anything except the energetic accumulation of past conditioning, our ideas, our fictions? Is this thing we call awareness any different? What is it?

Thinking, thinking, thinking.

At dawn I am waiting to see Toni.

Get ready for a blast of bad air, I plan to tell her, but instead—entering the meeting room—I am greeted by the fragrance of flowers.

"Well, it's quite pleasant in here," I say, surprised.

"Have you been having a hard time?" she asks.

"I've been in the bottomless pit." I laugh. "I'm laughing, but it's not funny," I tell her.

"Well, let's have a good laugh first," she says, smiling. And then she grows serious, listening.

"I know that the bottomless pit is nothing but a thought," I tell her, "and that I'm nothing but a hologram . . ."

"No, no, you're right here," she says, putting her hands firmly on my knees and laughing. "Without self-images we are *more* alive, not less alive. People imagine that if they don't have all these images, everything will be gray and lifeless, without any passion or joy. 'Will there still be sex?' they ask me." She laughs.

"You don't *surrender* the self," she says later. "It just happens, with awareness of the images. What is there without the images? Who called it nothing? Who said it was gray and lifeless? These are just ideas. The 'me' is the past and the future, memory and imagination. But what is it right here, right now?"

I tell her I feel hopeless. That there is no awareness. It's all just thoughts and images, layer after layer of thoughts and images.

"These are just more thoughts," she says. "Don't trust the thoughts. What's real is the sunrise, the footsteps, the smell of the flowers. We have our moods, like the weather. I don't want to encourage you. We don't need that. There's something much deeper available. Just to be here in this moment, without time. This is your whole life. This isn't some sideline activity. This is it—just to feel and be with what is."

I notice how she talks. Nothing is personalized. "There is wanting," she says, rather than "I wanted."

Sitting on my cushion, I visualize a huge hot-fudge sundae. I grow exhausted. Exhausted beyond exhaustion. Finally, I go through an hour-long struggle with myself about whether or not to leave the sitting room at the next break and take a nap—forbidden and wimpy behavior in the Zen tradition from which I come, but perfectly acceptable here. I finally conclude that my sole motivation for continuing to sit is to bolster my self-image and impress Toni if she happens to come in, not that I think Toni herself would actually be impressed by this; it is my projection of her that would be impressed. I leave and go take a nap. This is a huge breakthrough for me, as if some reservoir of energy has been freed up. That night I find myself sitting after the last sitting, something I have never done before, and have always found unimaginable.

A warm wind at dawn. Everyone is up and outside this morning before the first sitting, looking at the white moon setting into the hills, and Heather the cat is out, too, chasing bugs or phantoms or her tail, I'm not sure which, but she's having fun. Walking in the morning after breakfast, I pass baby rabbits everywhere vacuuming up the leaves. An owl flies just over my head through the trees.

In her talks, Toni seems to be defending the idea that there is no practice here. I sit on my cushion composing position papers in my head for hours about how there *is* a practice here. These thoughts constrict everything. I am no longer aware of birds and breezes. I feel completely identified with my position. The existence of an opposing or different position provokes fear, anger, feelings of separation and all the pain of that. I *know* I am right. It feels horrible.

Next thing I know, Toni and I are discussing self-defense. Is it ever necessary to fight back? What's wrong with self-defense and self-preservation? It's natural. If given the opportunity to kill Hitler, or one of these serial rapist-killers who torture and mutilate scores of women, shouldn't we take it? Is this any different from removing a cancer from the body? And yet maybe something is wrong with it, because I feel so rotten. I feel threatened. Hostile. Angry. I am defending myself. I have been doing this for years.

The retreat ends in four hours. Only four hours left to "get it." I feel terrible pressure and anxiety. What is it that we're trying so hard to get? The day is hot and humid. Sweat is pouring off my body as I sit. Suddenly this feral wind comes sweeping through the fields. Everything is moving. The sky goes dark and thunder crashes, lighting rips across the sky, rain pours down. The power goes off. And then it stops. The last period of the retreat is utterly calm. The air smells cool and sweet and fresh.

Can we be with what's happening right now? Toni asks. Not what *will* happen to us in the future, but what actually *is* right now this moment.

16

After the retreat, I am having dinner with Toni and her husband, Kyle, several of the people on staff and a bunch of people from the retreat. I am telling the story of my life, and hearing myself doing it, noticing the pride I take in it, the way I shape and embellish it, and suddenly I feel a little bit sickened by it. Something rings false.

A group of us watch videos of Krishnamurti in the evening, made at the very end of his life. I have never heard him before. To pursue nonviolence is a form of violence, he says, because when we pursue nonviolence it means that we are no longer attentive to what actually is, but are instead chasing after an idea. Attentive listening to what is has tremendous healing power. Just to *listen,* without trying to *do* anything.

Toni compares this work we're doing to the aliveness of a baby exploring the world. She doesn't call it practice, as they do in many schools of meditation, because to her that word automatically conveys ideas of effort and attainment—a self-improvement program, whereas awareness can never be objectified or made into a program.

David Steindl-Rast, a Catholic monk, talks in one of his

books about prayer as wholehearted attention, a state of mind that has two components: concentration, which is a narrowing down and focusing in, and wonderment, which is expansive and limitless. I remember him saying that wholehearted attention must paradoxically include both dimensions simultaneously.

Toni seems almost to be suggesting pure wonderment, without concentration, but she seems enormously concentrated. Perhaps the key lies in the realm of intention. Babies focus or concentrate on what interests or pleases them. As soon as a new interest emerges or appears, their focus will shift. Concentration thus arises naturally. It is spontaneous, alive, always moving. It is free. There is no resistance or effort. It is not a direction imposed by thought, some agenda of prescribed or forced behavior. Most meditation practices, on the other hand, are created and sustained by thought, and seem to reinforce the image of a self—a meditator—who is "doing" meditation, and getting somewhere spiritually through such discipline and effort.

The concentration of a baby is alive wonderment. It is to that kind of organic interest, or passion, and awareness that Toni seems to be pointing: listening that is not rote or methodical in any way. The baby has no sense yet of self-image, of itself as an object—a person—who needs to be improved, and Toni will question any meditation practice that contributes to such a picture.

She talks of taking her grandson on a walk at twilight in Rochester on a winter evening, and how he sat down in a pool of light in the snow under a streetlamp, just wanting to be there in that light. Was he "practicing" something? she asks.

It's an amazing process, this work. Intentions and formu-

las arise so quickly. Letting go of them all. And then there will
be nothing, we think, but who called it nothing? It is "the
green of the pines, the twist of the brambles . . . the red of the
flowers and the white of the snow" (Ryusui).

17

I attend a staff meeting, with every intention of just listening
and observing. But I become so ridiculously opinionated that
I cannot stop myself from speaking up. I watch how attached
I am to my opinions and their importance, how irritated and
threatened I feel by those whose views are different.

People here don't always look at each other when they are
talking, they seem subdued, and the process often appears
meandering and unfocused. It isn't the kind of meeting I'm
used to, where everyone makes eye contact and there's lots of
affect and an efficient facilitator speeds things along at a crisp
pace. I am instantly convinced that what I'm accustomed to is
better, that this is not so good. The judgments come so
quickly, the labels I slap onto other people or onto other—
unfamiliar—ways of behaving.

I feel separate from these people. They're mostly men;
I'm a woman. They're all straight; I'm gay. They're Easterners;
I'm a Westerner. They all have two hands; I have one. I have
a very strong "I'm Really Different" program. What is this
attachment to my separateness? This feeling of being different,
for whatever reason. Are any of these people here really so
different from me? Do they feel any less separate? Why do I
cling to various identities? Why do I feel as though no one
really knows me until they know my life story? Tremendous
fear arises at the thought of losing my labels, and at the same

time there is immense peace in living without them, which is part of what happens on a silent retreat.

One of Toni's talks at the California retreat was about the roots of war in these separations we create and defend: my country, my subculture, my group, my belief, my story. It was the first time I felt something in me open up to the idea of going beyond self-defense, on both the personal and global levels.

Can I really stop defending myself? Defending women? Defending the environment? Is there some other way to do it? Some other way to stop brutalizing the earth and each other, to liberate all of us? This feels dangerous and scary. I don't want to be unresponsive to suffering and injustice.

We habitually want answers to questions. We want resolutions, endings, conclusions. Toni suggests the possibility of keeping the question itself alive in the mind, unanswered, open. We search desperately for solutions to our problems, she says, but the only real solution is to be with the problem. Not analytically, but immediately. To really *see* the problem.

I see how much dogmatism, divisiveness, and arrogance there is in political thinking much—maybe most—of the time; how narrow-minded people get. I see that a violent, opinionated approach will never end conflict and injustice.

This isn't to say that political work should be abandoned or that it accomplishes nothing at all. I've often said that I owe my life to politics, that if it hadn't been for the women's and gay liberation movements coming on the scene when they did, I would have gone to my death at the bar where I drank. But I became locked into so many positions about everything. Everything became black and white, us and them. How easily we human beings polarize things, creating enemies in the name of a new and better world. The truth is so much messier, so much more difficult to swallow. Maybe the point isn't to let go of politics or political insight, but simply to see more clearly what we're doing, to listen without conclusions. Is that possible?

There is so much pressure to keep each of my identities, each of my labels intact. I think of all the pressure from the twelve-step programs to wear those chosen addict labels for the rest of your life, the pressure in minority communities to identify yourself with the group. And in majority groups the same thing happens so automatically and on such a wide-spread level that it goes mostly unnoticed—one is *presumed* to be white, heterosexual, or able-bodied, and if you whisper anything contrary to that, people ask you why you're flaunting it.

Toni, on the other hand, questions *all* labels and images of who we are. She points to something beyond merely replacing negative images with positive ones. Flattery is as destructive as deprecation, she says. They go together like the two sides of a coin.

I told Toni how much her work scared me because I've worked so hard to get beyond the self-hatred and silencing of myself that comes from growing up female, disabled, and bi-sexual in a patriarchal society, and I'm afraid that if I really let go into what she's talking about, this seeing through all images—of my self, even!—that all this progress I've made will be lost.

"You're afraid you'll go back to how you were in the past?" she asked.

I nodded.

Her eyes lit up and she laughed her wonderful, warm

laugh. "But you won't," she said emphatically. "Of course you won't!"

❀

Perhaps there *is* something outside of conditioning. I've gone for days since the retreat without biting my fingers—an addictive habit I've had since childhood, and on the plane flight back to California I just sat there, without reading or writing or anything, not because I decided to do this, but simply because it happened. There was no need of anything, no desire at all to move away from presence. No fear.

18

I imagined that I was done with Zen forever. But then I did a sesshin in California with Maurine Stuart, a Zen roshi from Massachusetts who was terminally ill at the time. And I found myself going back—after Maurine—to the Berkeley Zen Center. I told Mel that I wanted to be his student again and sew a rakusu and take the precepts. A rakusu is one of those little Buddhist robes that looks like a bib. At the Berkeley Zen Center you sew your own. You have to cut a big piece of dark cloth into little pieces and sew them back together again, saying a mantra with each stitch, one word as the needle goes in and another word as the needle comes out. Then the teacher presents the finished robe to you in a formal ceremony along with a Buddhist name, and you take the precepts, which are sort of like the Ten Commandments, except you aren't supposed to think of them that way.

I knew in my body that I was taking a false turn sewing

that rakusu. But the fantasy behind it was compelling, so I kept going. I could see myself as a priest.

A year went by. I sat with Joko Beck again, and with Toni in California. I sewed. I obsessed about moving to Springwater. And finally I put my unfinished rakusu aside, packed up my things, and, in the autumn of 1989, off I went. I was going to Springwater for six months as a volunteer, which meant room and board in exchange for work.

"You're going to northwestern New York for the winter?!" someone asked incredulously.

I moved to the middle of nowhere, a place tourists would avoid at all costs—northwestern New York, the foothills of the Midwest. And now here I am in a place with ice storms and deerflies and mosquitoes, living with a bunch of heterosexual men.

Perfect.

19

*I make films to occupy my time. If I were strong enough
to do nothing, I wouldn't do anything at all. It's because
I'm not strong enough to do nothing that I make films.
There isn't any other reason.
There is nothing truer I can say about my enterprise.*

MARGUERITE DURAS

Is it Toni who sits beside me late at night in the meditation room? I feel the reactions in my body to her imagined presence: tightening gut, constricted throat, fast breathing, energy shooting through me.

I want to impress her: appear suave, cool, grounded, and wise. I don't want to be the nervously gulping, heavily breathing person that I am at this moment. I try to conceal my gulping and breathing.

"The most important book to read is yourself," Toni says. "If you read that book, you will have read all the others."

I see the ideas and images about this person beside me, the reactions in my body, the urge to become somebody, to be done with who I am right now. Endless thoughts and the chemical reactions, sensations, and emotions they produce. Maybe "I" am not doing any of this. Maybe it is just happening. Like the wind.

What am I, this moment, without any images at all?

Darkness and breath, writing a journal. There is no sense in it, only sensation. The airplane in the night sky passing through the tissues of my body, waves of sound and light, heart beating, deer snorting in the woods. My fingers on paper. Words. Scat. Pictures in the mind.

I wonder about the urge to write, to put my life into words, to make sense out of the sensations, to create a product. Perhaps the most beautiful offering is silence.

These journals seem to embody the fictional storyline about "me" that we all keep creating, on paper or in our heads, convincing ourselves and each other of its reality. We create and recreate ourselves through this practice of storytelling. Joan, who has one arm, is a lesbian, or a bisexual, an ex-drunk, an addict, a former leftist radical, a writer, a meditator, a person. At times, my writing seems like a monstrosity of narrational memory that I am lugging around like some kind of Samuel Beckett character, unable to put it down.

So should I throw it into the furnace in a Final Act of Liberation? Or should I buckle down and finish a book once and for all, since—as Mel told me—nirvana is seeing one thing through to completion? I contemplate both possibilities: a published book or these pages blazing up and disappearing, freeing me from this story that I think is mine to live and tell about, over and over again. But of course, even this is another story: thought imagining a "me" who would be better (holier, freer, happier) without these words, without this book, without this story.

"The birds aren't worried about why they're singing," Paul says to me.

Writing is an offering: to share, to clarify, to play. I want to describe the pain in order to see it, in order to heal, in order to realize wholeness—because everyone has this arm of mine in some form or another, everyone is queer in some way, everyone has this same human mind, albeit we each have our particular psychological furnishings—one person is afraid to go out and another is afraid to stay in.

Writing is a way of listening, a way of changing perception. It seems there is something worthwhile in telling our stories, bringing to light and sharing what has been hidden or silenced, what has long existed in secrecy. It breaks down isolation and conditioning. This kind of sharing reveals how common our darkest secrets really are—and it also helps us understand other people's experiences, which may be different from our own. An addictive, non-democratic society is built on lies and secrets, on disowned shadow parts and excluded minorities, and hearing the whole truth is important.

But what is the truth? Toni's work keeps that question always alive in the midst of such speaking and sharing. And I see more clearly the enormous need to talk personally, about "me," to tell my story, to be somebody, to produce something. And so, I don't know. I write. I listen. I wonder.

"Can a particular human life be looked at and exposed impersonally—meaning without identifying with it?" Toni asked. "Is that possible? Find out!" she said.

20

Huge migrations are heading south. A wild honking in the treetops growing louder and louder, until geese pass overhead, with a wind that feels like winter. My fingers are stiff. Red orange yellow leaves blow past, branches growing bare. The sky darkens as white-tailed deer spring and leap through the tall grass into the forest of wet bark and leaves, a steamy place full of weather. There are sudden rains and clearings, cold shrieking winds. Wild turkeys rise from a field. The chilling cry of an owl goes through my bones, with the rustling leaves blown into silence.

I have discovered that Toni can be fussy, unimaginative, and quite ordinary, that she's entirely capable of being an unspectacular, irritating, regular person. I wanted her to be perfect, and there is something frightening and disturbing in the discovery that she is not.

Toni wants to be seen as a friend. But our relationships with her are not exactly like a friendship between peers, at least not always, at least not in my experience. I feel I am in the student position in most of our formal transactions. I do her laundry and clean her apartment as part of my job here. She never comes to my room to hang out like a regular friend; if I want to see her alone, I do so mostly by appointment. She is certainly the guiding force here at Springwater.

For years, in feminism and radical therapy, I fought for the recognition of material conditions and power imbalances. The therapist was always subjective and biased, never neutral and objective as traditional psychotherapy had claimed. And now I hear Toni saying she has no power, no bias, no point of view, and my danger signals go off. But maybe I'm stuck in old battles, old constructs, old tapes. Truth is fluid and moving. Didn't Suzuki Roshi say that the secret of Zen is "Not Always So"? Sometimes I can't find the problem anymore. It vanishes, because the problem is all thought.

Paul and I talk. What is going on when we get into this mode of tearing apart the teacher, being critical of Toni? He gets into this mode sometimes himself, he says. How is it that we make something out of this "teacher," something to revere or critique, depending on our mood? Why is there this need to focus on personality and then confuse that with the teaching itself?

I like Paul. I am seeing him more spaciously. It is dusk and the room where we sit is growing darker and darker as we talk. We are disappearing.

There is some desire for teachers to be completely perfect, completely likable, so that we can turn our life over to them. We hope they can save us.

A few of us have talked about the possibility of doing a

seven-day retreat without a teacher. No meetings, no talks, no tapes, no one who is presumed to know. Remove the authority completely. I wonder what that would be like?

Would it remove the authority? Or does Toni, through her talking and meeting with us, actually remove it in a much more vital way? What is "Toni," after all?

21

I spent the whole seven days of the October retreat being critical of Toni, seeing the cracks, the flaws, everything I don't like. Her talks bored me, and it seemed that she was giving essentially the same series of talks over again. Her vision appeared simplistic and naive. I kept hearing the Toni Packer Party Line, and the denial of its existence: the dogma of no-dogma.

It disturbs me when I hear Toni saying that it's possible to be beyond conditioning, free from memory. Because the minute we begin to think, talk, or listen to others, we are in the realm of language, and therefore of memory and conditioning. Even the way we see shapes and colors is conditioned and remembered, as Toni knows, because she has said so. What, then, does she mean by "truth"? What is there outside the constantly shifting interactions of text and reader, text and writer, text and text?

I get the feeling that Krishnamurti actually thinks he's in such an unconditioned state most of the time. And yet I see his political ideas, his prejudices, his arrogant attitude toward people at times. I see that his photograph is on the cover of every one of his books, and it seems obvious to me that he had conditioning and that he had an ego. It frightens me that Toni seems to regard Krishnamurti as being totally clear, that she doesn't seem to see his arrogance. Why does it frighten me? It frightens me because I want her to hand me the answers. The right answers.

"These are such important questions, Joan," Toni says to me, "not just to put to oneself discursively and then move on with other thoughts, but to hold in the mind and let discovery happen in the light of the questions."

I feel afraid of her simplicity, and bent upon disproving her. And in that, there is no space to listen. I wonder, is she deluding herself? Subscribing to some pie-in-the-sky belief that she has transcended memory and conditioning, and is miraculously able to "look freshly" with her sixty-some-year-old brain? Isn't "looking freshly" just another frame, another idea? Another ideal?

Toni listens to me so intently, and then she closes her eyes. "Can one tell whether one—or someone else—is speaking out of the clarity of insight, or if they are deluding themselves?" she asks. "Is it possible to see the difference between the expression of belief, frame, idea, ideal, and an expression which does not come out of those?"

There is a long silence. Birds sing. "Beyond just voicing skepticism," she continues, "can one actually *see* delusion as a fact, in oneself as well as others?"

I hate that word *fact.* I ask her what she means by it.

"I mean perception which is not distorted and fragmented by the pressures of self-centeredness. In the absence of the mental-emotional-physical pressure of self-centeredness (on all levels of consciousness—not just the surface), perception changes. It is not bound by thought and its accompaniments. There is no separation between a 'me' and the wholeness of life. This is not a belief, Joan. And it is not particular to me or Krishnamurti or anyone else.

"I'm not implying that someone speaking out of a state of seeing is forever incapable of deluding themselves. In insight there is no delusion, but the instant there is inattention the self-structure is in operation. Words and language are always limited, but is there something that is not?"

"Don't believe anyone," she says later, "including one's own ideas!"

But I keep arguing with her.

"What do you want from me?" she asks.

I want her to be the Perfect Teacher.

Watching how the mind works: If Toni can't be the Perfect Teacher, then who can? Katagiri Roshi! Of course! I'll try Katagiri Roshi next! I spend days plotting out my trip to Minnesota, my new life at the Minnesota Zen Center.

What is it that I want this Perfect Teacher to tell me? What is it that I'm racing all over the world trying to hear?

I was grappling with this question of authority all during the retreat, deconstructing it, probing it, peeling it away. By the end, I felt as though I had no teacher, that there is no teacher anywhere, that all any of us has is the silence, the listening, the attention to this moment.

When there is listening, none of this matters. It isn't even real. It's all a game of the mind. A huge invention of thought spinning itself out in wider and wider circles away from the point.

You must see clearly that there is really nothing at all.

HUANG PO

During the final period of the retreat, a neighboring church began to play Christmas carols on their bells, very loud, over and over and over. This was in October. They were rehearsing. "O Little Town of Bethlehem." "Hark! The Herald Angels Sing." Despite my efforts to push it away or "listen freshly," I was rigid and tight and seething with wanting the bells to shut up and stop ruining our perfectly silent retreat. And there were gunshots, from the hunters in the woods. The sky grew stormy and dark. "O Little Town of Bethlehem." *Bang bang.* Tense up. Resist. Resist. It was the perfect finale.

It is my mother's eightieth birthday the next day. I call her up.

"I'm very wise now," she jokes, "in case you have any questions."

"What is it all about? What's the point?" I ask.

"To have fun!" she replies. "To enjoy!"

This is the last thing that would ever occur to me.

My mother has been reading Joseph Campbell. Follow your bliss, she tells me. I feel that my bliss is being right here, in silence, doing nothing at all. But there are fears: Maybe being here means I failed to make it "out there" in the "real" world.

But who decided that retreat centers are not "the real world"? Here we are on the verge of nuclear holocaust and environmental annihilation, and I'm worried about being successful in the so-called "real world"!?

I call my friend Elaine in San Francisco. What is life all about? she asks. Living a life so that our names can go on some giant roll call in the heavens: She paid her rent, she paid her taxes, she wrote her books? Shit, Elaine says, I'd rather be on a list of people who ate as many pot stickers as they wanted to.

22

Toni calls a meeting of the entire staff after the retreat to discuss the questions I raised about the existence and denial of form, hierarchy, and authority at Springwater, and the attitude of superiority over people practicing in more traditional ways. My stomach sinks. I can't even remember what I think.

We sit in a circle, and I am trembling and cold and headachy. My jaw is tight. It's hard to listen, my thoughts and sensations are so strong. Sometimes I don't hear at all what is said. After the meeting, I am still shaky and everyone is in the kitchen, and Toni asks me how it was for me to be the focus of so much of the meeting, and I tell her I'm cold and trembling, and she says, yes . . . she feels that way, too.

Toni has to deal with everyone's transferences and projections, wanting her to be perfect, or different, challenging every word she says or swooning at her feet. Why not look toward our working together in a common effort, instead of thinking in terms of "accepting" or "rejecting" her as someone to imitate or follow?

It is such an ancient pattern for me always to be looking for the perfect life: the perfect career, the perfect relationship, the perfect teacher, the perfect place to live, and to split as soon as the inevitable imperfections and inadequacies become apparent. I see how little love there is in such an approach. I don't want to do this with Toni and Springwater. Somehow, it feels important to hang in there, to make it through this process. My whole body-mind senses that this is the truth. This work I am doing here feels right to me. And beyond all this noise of words and doubts there is something much more profound. Something words can't touch. Something very, very simple.

Being here seems to entail a process of questioning everything, and of being thrown back upon myself, to look inward instead of seeking the solutions externally. I often find myself filled with fear that no one likes me, wanting attention and reassurance, and being pushed just to be there with that feeling and see it, instead of trying to get reinforcement externally. There is a feeling of absolute loneliness and isolation that is probably at the bottom of all my addictions. The fear of being separate. The fear that others don't like me, don't see me accurately, that I'm all alone. There is an urge to cover this fear with something—food, sex, entertainment, drugs, alcohol, thinking—or else to have other people show and tell me that they love me, they want me. I am beginning to discover that I engineer all kinds of subtle manipulations to weasel such reassurances out of others. I never saw it before. But I'm doing it all the time. Instead of sitting with the fear, the loneliness, the discomfort—listening to it, going all the way to the root of it.

"You have to go for broke in this work," Sharon tells me. I think of Mel: "In Zen you have to burn all your bridges so you can't go back."

23

The moon is almost full the night the November retreat begins. Feelings of fear, anxiety, anticipation, and excitement sweep over me. We settle into the silence, the not-knowing. Toni's talks seem brilliant. I feel completely open to her. All the problems I was having with her are gone and there is tremendous appreciation for the way she imposes nothing at all, her questioning of all effort.

On the third night, I meet with her. It is Toni's last meeting for that day. It's late. She's tired and so am I. There is a white orchid on the table beside us. Everything is alive, electric, whole. Toni, Joan, orchid, wind, moonlight, all breathing together, listening.

And then suddenly thought turns Toni into the authority figure, the teacher, and I begin talking about myself and what I should do with my life, wanting Toni to provide the answers. I feel the aliveness of our connection die. I'm using her, projecting onto her, not listening anymore.

I am full of self-hate afterward, as if "I" had somehow produced these thoughts. I toss and turn with nightmares. Someone in the next room wakes up screaming. I hear her roommate comforting her. The hours tick by. I lie awake biting my fingers in the darkness, unable to stop.

The next morning when I meet with Toni I speak to her about this horrible addiction. It may sound trivial, but I bite the flesh, not the nails, often drawing blood, and I can get so mesmerized by it that I cannot bring myself to stop. I am thus virtually paralyzed, often for hours at a time, chewing on my hand, unable to stop, unable to do anything else, my entire body in a spasm of tension. The whole experience feels both numbing and torturous, and inevitably fills me with self-hatred and shame. I've tried every imaginable cure and nothing has worked.

Toni listens, and suggests not trying to get rid of it! Simply be with it, she says. What is it? How does it feel? What are the thoughts, including the desire to stop, the belief that I can't, the judgments of myself. Experience the sensations in my jaw, my fingers, my shoulder, my stomach, hear the sounds in the room. Just listen, to the *whole* thing, without judgment.

"Can *all* of this be allowed to reveal itself?" Toni asks. "You can't impose improvements," she says. "With willpower comes resistance. Check it out for yourself."

How exactly did "I" stop drinking, doing drugs, or smoking cigarettes? There were numerous attempts that failed, and then there was success. How did that happen? What shifted? Is there a person here, a "me," who is capable of deciding to stop an addictive pattern? And, if so, why doesn't it always work? Why do some people succeed and others fail? Why is it that someone like me, who has successfully let go of many addictive behaviors, is still biting my fingers? Why don't I stop? What brings a person to the point of stopping?

Habit has two parts, Toni says. There is the habit itself (finger biting, smoking, drinking, whatever), and there is the observer who wants to stop, who is also a habit. And there is the conflict, the battle between the desire to indulge, which is an escape from what is, and the desire to stop, which is also a movement away from what is.

Toni suggests that the only real solution lies in complete awareness. In such awareness there is no chooser who is "doing" the habitual behavior or the stopping, there is no program, no will, no intention, no judgment, no conflict, no separation from the problem, no self to be improved or fixed, no direction. It is open, relaxed seeing.

"Can we look carefully at this 'me' that seems to be the power behind making decisions, really go into it, trace this chooser, this doer, all the way to the root?" Toni asks me.

When we do that together, all we find is thoughts. Conflicting thoughts: "I want to bite," "I want to stop." It feels like a battle between "me-the-observer" and "me-the-addict." But both of these "me's" are images constructed by thought and imagination. What's actually going on is just an alternating, conflicting series of thoughts. No one is "doing" them; they're happening.

"I have to bite," "I can't stop," "I should stop," "I'm addicted," "I'm an addict," "I'm a terrible person," "How can I stop?" "If I just get this one loose end, then I'll be satiated," "It would be unbearable to feel what I would feel if I stopped," "I'm stuck, this is hopeless," "It's been going on for a long time," "It's out of control," "I'll never get free," "I should be able to control myself," "This is sick," "I want to be healthy."

"These are all *thoughts,*" Toni says. "Do you see that?"

"But some of them are true," I reply.

"Are they?" she asks with electric intensity, her eyes closed, her hands suspended in midair, listening.

"Well, I *am* addicted. It *is* out of control," I insist.

"Thought *seems* to be just reporting the facts, objectively: 'I'm addicted, this is out of control.' But are these really facts? Or are they ideas? These are very powerful thoughts, and every thought produces neurochemical reactions in the body."

Whichever position has more energy in that moment

wins out, Toni suggests, and then there is either the thought, "I'm good because I had the willpower to stop," or "I'm a failure because I didn't have enough willpower to stop." Thought creates "me" who has "done" one thing or the other, and is "successful" or "unsuccessful" as a result. And then more thoughts quickly follow: "I'm on my way to enlightenment" or "I'm a hopeless case on my way to total doom." Either of these thought-trains will generate a tremendous response in the body, either good feelings or terrible feelings, elation or depression.

"Do you see how all these powerful thoughts and the feelings they produce in the body all revolve around the idea and image of 'me'?" Toni asks. "Do you see how it's all thinking?"

There is rain falling outside the meeting room, trickling down the window.

I see that in this work there is no attempt whatsoever to pass judgment on what is, cut it off, control it, discipline it, change it. There is simply attention. Attention that is gone as soon as it is sought after or named. It comes and goes. There is nothing to do. But be diligent about doing nothing, Zen master Huang Po advises in one of the passages Toni reads to us on the last day of every retreat.

Rain turns to snow and back to rain again. The air is cold and smells of wet leaves, moisture, and mulch, the last wild apples. Sweet and pungent. The trees are bare and there is a thin skin of ice on the surface of the pond at dawn.

Dinner after retreat ends seems astonishingly noisy. The silence broken, eye contact and conversation restored. The words again, the boxes, the stories, the labels, the costumes. What do you do? Where do you live? Have you done this before? Everyone's faces are clear and luminous. There is so much love after a week in silence. So much has shifted, invisibly and without effort.

I'm aware of myself being seductive, wanting attention. I never thought of myself as seductive before I began working with Toni. But it's going on so much of the time. Charming people, flattering them, assuaging them, winning them over, magnetizing them, wanting them to like me. I hear myself being too loud, not listening to the others, caught up in my stories. Seeing all this, I watch thought judging and condemning me, the harshness of it. I am no good. I see how this constant image-making destroys the actual living connection between human beings.

Out of seeing, amazing shifts do seem to occur. But if we try to create shifts, to free ourselves, then we only get more and more entangled in our efforts.

I talked to my friend Frank on the phone that evening. Frank used to live in Vermont and would come to Springwater occasionally for retreats, and then he moved out to California to be a cook, which is where I met him.

"I was at work chopping onions yesterday," he says, "and suddenly I was filled with sadness . . . because here I am, I've got my dream, exactly what I wanted, I'm working at the restaurant I wanted to be at, I have a terrific place to live, and suddenly I was really sad because now I just have to chop the onions, you know?"

Isn't that exactly it? Chopping the onions.

24

It is winter now in northwestern New York. I love being in the country. Don't want to return to city living. Deer-hunting season I could have done without, but at least I did survive it. We wear orange vests in the woods to avoid being shot.

The grief in Toni's eyes the night the deer was killed by the pond. A hunter had wounded it, and tracked it onto center land to finish it off. Toni and I sat facing each other in the meeting room, listening to the rain.

"The rain is nice," I say.

"Um," she replies. "It washes away the blood."

Rain turning back into snow. And in the morning, no trace of death, except in our minds.

I love the fresh air, nature, silence. Such a pervasive, wondrous quiet. The relief of a life without date books and appointment calendars, without the constant interruptions of phone calls and activities, all that delicious sound and fury, in which my energy gets so easily dissipated and scattered. The pages of my once-jammed date book are blank. I go for months at a time without ever riding in a car or walking on concrete. I like being in a place where social interactions occur spontaneously, organically, instead of being planned days or weeks or months in advance. Life at Springwater is focused and still in some way, healing.

I think some of it has to do with the structure and rhythm of daily work, especially when that work is manual labor, which I find satisfying. Cleaning toilets and scrubbing walls. Mostly I do housekeeping—vacuuming the floors, dusting the furniture, washing the windows. During non-retreat times, we work five days a week from eight-thirty in the morning until four-thirty in the afternoon, with a generous hour for lunch. One afternoon a week we have a staff meeting that frequently lasts into the early evening. Other than that, our time is mostly unstructured. Everyone takes turns making breakfast for the group. Lunch is our main meal and is prepared for us—on workdays—by the kitchen person. We all make our own supper, and everyone participates in dishwashing. People work hard at their jobs here—many work overtime—but the atmosphere is relaxed and no one is looking askance if a breakfast conversation runs over into work hours and things start a few minutes late, or someone knocks off early.

Springwater offers a unique opportunity to be quiet in nature without a highly structured program being imposed on you in the process. It offers *nothing,* which is something increasingly hard to come upon in our culture. We are used to tremendous stimulation and speed, efficiency and purposefulness.

A few people on staff don't sit at all anymore, and read novels and magazines during the retreats. I was shocked when I first discovered this. I have come to see, though, that meditation in the true sense does not depend on sitting, although sitting may be helpful. Here, where there is freedom of choice in such matters, there is none of the athletic endurance quality so present in Zen practice, except to the degree that those of us who come out of that tradition have internalized it and bring it along with us. I'm not opposed to this endurance trip. For me it was useful to sit through everything without moving, without the option to go for a long walk instead. I learned from that.

But at this point, I find that it's not necessarily so useful to approach it in such a rigorous way. I don't mean to imply that it isn't still a vital practice for me to sit through disturbance, because it is, but I notice that it doesn't have to happen by being motionless in the lotus posture. And in fact, sitting like that can become a kind of subtle, or not-so-subtle, reinforcement of the very heart of the problem: the sense of "me." I remember how I prided myself on being able to sit through long periods at the Zen center without ever moving at all. When I first got here, I prided myself on being at every sitting. I wanted "practice" to be as demanding as possible, the harder the better.

I'm appreciating the chance to work in a different way, a way that questions those aspects of what can so easily become self-image and effort to get somewhere and become somebody. Of course, such questioning and insight can presumably also occur in the midst of traditional Zen rigor, but Toni's way seems to make it much more easily visible, interrupting the old patterns as completely as she does, calling them into question.

I have noticed this past year that it is infinitely easier to sit on my cushion officially Doing Nothing than to sit in an armchair really doing nothing. I sit quite happily on my cushion every day "meditating," at least an hour, often more, no problem. But to sit in an armchair actually doing nothing at all, well, I can tolerate that about five minutes a week.

This last retreat, I experimented with sitting part of the time in a chair. Back at the Zen center, we were encouraged to sit on meditation cushions in some form of lotus posture. While it was permissible to sit in a chair if you had some kind of "problem," it was unmistakable that the "correct" and "best" posture for meditation was on that cushion. It was amazing to see everything that came up when I hauled that chair into the sitting room. I can remember long ago at the Zen center when I'd see people who had to sit in chairs because of back problems; thinking to myself that if I ever had to do that, I'd give up Zen. It wouldn't be real Zen if I was in a chair! And now, here I was, in a chair. Sitting there in that chair, myriad self-images and injunctions came into awareness and lost their authority, something loosened and released.

Years ago when I went through primal therapy, we had to spend three weeks in a room without doing anything at all, including talking, reading, writing, sleeping during the day, eating between meals, smoking, nail-biting, masturbating, yoga, exercising, or meditating—and by meditating, they meant some kind of formal practice—not because all those things are *necessarily* escapes, but they *can* be, and so to confront us totally with our discomfort, they were all removed. It was quite revealing. It also interests me that I was able, for those three weeks, to suspend willingly my seemingly uncontrollable addictions at the time: finger-biting and smoking.

I can see now that sometimes being there in the sitting room in that ancient and sanctioned position, it is almost impossible *not* to think that I'm doing something. So I'm wondering about it: What is meditation, really?

Do Zen and Toni make fundamentally different assumptions about what happens if rules and forms are stripped away? Zen thinking that, given a chance, people will take the easy way out, and Toni seeing that without anything imposed, intelligence and wisdom will emerge?

25

One interesting topic under discussion has been the question of what will happen to Springwater after Toni's death. Not that her death is expected anytime soon—it isn't—but she is in her sixties and others on staff are realizing that they are getting older as well, and so the question begins to arise. I first heard it come up at a recent trustee meeting where Toni announced that she no longer plans to name a successor, and since then the topic has come up at a staff meeting, and in many informal discussions, and seems to trigger interesting and important questions.

First, there is my disappointment. I wanted to be her successor. I suppose the image of oneself as the teacher is a fairly common one, although I haven't heard many people admit to it. When Roshi Kapleau asked Toni to take over the Rochester Zen Center, she was apparently terribly unhappy. I guess that's the difference between me and someone who's qualified for the job.

Of course, if Toni actually turned to me—not in fantasy, but in real life—and said, "I want you to take over Springwater," I guess I'd be pretty unhappy, too. I mean, what a nightmare. But in fantasy, it can sound very appealing.

What makes a teacher? I wonder. Does Toni think about sharing her function and finding ways for others to learn teaching skills? Are they skills that can be learned? Is it that no one who is working with her is spiritually mature enough to begin to take on the work of giving talks and having meetings? If that's true, how does that change?

At some of the Zen centers where I've been, it seems as

80

though you go through a training program to become a teacher. It's not much different from becoming a doctor or a therapist or an auto mechanic. New teachers are sprouting up everywhere. But realization is not something you get through "training," and Toni seems to feel that any kind of program or track designed to prepare someone to take over her "job" would be the ultimate misunderstanding of her work. Becoming a teacher or making someone into a teacher because a person needs a career and/or because an institution needs a person to fill that role—or in order to keep a particular organization or tradition alive—is a dangerously mechanical approach, and runs contrary to everything Springwater is about.

Should Springwater continue beyond Toni's death? Why do we want it to continue? Is it because we actually *see* the importance of the work here? How much has to do with our own desire (not necessarily bad) to have an enduring place to live, a community in which to grow old and retire, a career with definite ranks we can progress through, something apparently stable and secure with which we can identify ourselves and to which we can belong: a tradition, a lineage, a guarantee of immortality?

Creating an institution or organization of any kind around meditative work is a very delicate affair, even in a case like this, where there is tremendous commitment to avoiding authoritarian tradition and exposing all forms of identification and image-making. As Toni says, "It gives one a feeling of importance and security to be identified with something larger, greater than oneself, and therefore this something assumes great importance." It is so easy to confuse the institution with the inquiry, to become idolatrous.

Do you have the essence? Toni asks. If you have the

essence, the future will emerge. Toni speaks of the future unfolding organically, from the grass roots up, rather than from the top down. It can't be planned, she says. The urge to plan it comes from clutching. And then you create something artificial: hierarchies, career ladders, systems, traditions, and all the rest. Everything she has worked so hard to avoid. You have to stay open. See what happens.

Toni says she hopes the center will continue to operate as a meditation and retreat center after she is gone. It would be great to keep alive a place for this work, for retreats, for being quiet in nature, for meeting with others who are similarly engaged and interested. If the importance and value of this is actually seen and felt, with genuine passion, then one will act accordingly, not merely talk and think and worry about it instead. And out of that kind of lucid action things do happen. The money comes, the people come, things happen as needed. That's how Springwater got here in the first place. Not because people sat around wondering if it was possible or worrying about what would become of it if Toni died.

I sometimes wonder if there is something in the very structure here that blocks this kind of unfolding and maturing. Many Zen teachers I've known, including Joko and Maurine, and many other spiritual teachers, including Krishnamurti, have been outspoken in not wanting to create residential communities around their work. Some have said that such communities tend to attract immature and troubled people, and then encourage dependencies. You get room and board, there is the absence of certain pressures, demands, consequences that you'd find out in the "real" world.

Residential centers by their very nature do in some ways tend to resemble halfway houses and may attract people who need shelter, or feed into people's tendency to want to be taken care of, and this is certainly a pitfall if it is catered to. Your shopping, food preparation, and cleaning is done for you. It's virtually impossible to be fired. And there's Toni, this sort of Parent Figure, whether she wants to be or not, and perhaps at times a kind of family dynamic in which staff become "the kids."

The situation may inadvertently promote an abdication of autonomy or responsibility on the part of staff people by keeping them in some kind of infantile, intermediate zone where they need Toni to be complete. I feel it in myself here, this avoidance of full responsibility. I expect more of Toni than I do of myself. In seeing this as it arises, does it disappear? Or does it persist? Is it possible to create a community without an authority figure, where people remain alive and autonomous? Is it possible to do this with "Toni" still here, still teaching?

I can get so absorbed in worrying about all of this or in being self-righteous about my latest theories that I miss the truth, which is really so totally available and effortless. When I see it, there's no problem.

In the meeting room one night during the last retreat, I picked up a seashell from the table and held it to my ear.

"It says nothing," I reported, and put it back on the table.

Toni picked it up, held it to her ear for a long time, her face full of wonder, like a child . . . listening.

26

If only we could all realize how common our minds are, how innocently conditioned and utterly impersonal the whole process is. It would solve all our human problems. If we did something "wrong" (the language we use is loaded already with judgment), we would notice it as an interesting phenomenon that was off-base in some way, without having to deny it to ourselves or others, or pretend that it didn't really happen, all of which we do because we identify the behavior in question as "me" and we want our imaged "self" to be perfect and good. If other people criticized us or got angry at us, even if they did it in a terrible, hostile way, we would view their behavior as another interesting manifestation of energy, rather than as an attack on "me." This shift in perspective would have enormous implications on the global scale.

The thought may come up that "seeing impersonally" sounds heartless. But actually, the more I investigate it, the more it seems that following and believing thoughts is what's truly heartless. It's automatic and mechanical behavior, whereas not identifying with the thought-constructed storyline, and not taking things personally, is awakening to something much more creative.

27

Only in seeing and dropping unequivocally everything that divides us can there be freedom.

Toni Packer

Living in community is an adventure I like a lot, although it is not as easy as living with my Well-Chosen, Like-Minded Friends in the Bay Area. Zen teacher Bill Kwong said, "When you select your own friends they usually perpetuate your own delusions. But in a community you are stuck with each other. This is the difficulty and the richness of community."

Relationships reveal to us very quickly where we're attached. In isolation, one can create the illusion of enlightenment much more easily, I think. Coming from the Bay Area to a small rural community of mostly straight men where I am the only woman apart from Sharon, the only gay person, and the only disabled person living and working here is both upsetting and transformative.

My friends back home are mostly women, many are gay, most are writers or artists of some kind, quite a few are therapists. We share a cultural history, a social context, a common meaning. We speak the same language, have similar assumptions about the world. Being here at Springwater is a little bit like going to live in a foreign country. I have been removed from the web in which I have lived for most of my adult life. There is no one here who instantly gets lesbian humor or has the shared perspective you develop with people after twenty years in the same complex urban community.

On the other hand, there is a quiet simplicity here that I don't find in the Bay Area. There is less enrapturement with mental hot air. Things are slower and quieter. There is a spareness here that I love.

Still, I often feel alone. People watch videos of movies that I never want to see and most social events culminate in front of the television. Paul plays his rock music down below and my room vibrates, Roger belches loudly in the hallway outside my door. This is not always the quiet monastery I have long imagined. At times it feels more like living in a men's dormitory than a spiritual retreat center. I want a community without television, where no one would ever belch loudly or play rock music. I want a community that eats macrobiotically, a community with more women in it, more gay people. But, of course, surprise, surprise, this isn't the Perfect Place that I imagine. There is no Perfect Place, and the search for it is the root of all imperialist expansion and empire.

If Springwater were the way I think I want it to be, I'd undoubtedly complain about that, too. Fortunately there is some awareness that this is all very funny. And some desire to stop running, to stop my frantic search for perfection and self-improvement, to allow myself to *be* where I am with all its contradictions, to see the thoughts and feelings, the desires and aversions that arise, and not be moved by all that vast hysteria. To know finally that the "answer" I'm so desperately seeking is truly right here this moment and nowhere else. Where else could it possibly be?

My mind, of course, is always busy spinning other plans: other centers, other teachers, other landscapes, other lifestyles. Where to go next. I have this feeling that if I could just stay here, no matter what, at least for now, it would be so freeing. To paraphrase Reb Anderson, a teacher I worked with at the San Francisco Zen Center: Enlightenment is when Iowa is empty of Iowa and you can be in Iowa with all the problems of Iowa without wanting to be anyplace else.

Sometimes I even have rare moments of fondness and appreciation for the belching men and the rock music, of seeing them as the Buddha itself.

> *It is clinging to the false that makes the true so difficult to see. Once you understand that the false needs time and what needs time is false, you are nearer the*

Reality, which is timeless, ever in the now. . . . Reality is what makes the present so vital, so different from the past and future, which are merely mental. If you need time to achieve something, it must be false. The real is always with you; you need not wait to be what you are. Only you must not allow your mind to go out of yourself in search.

NISARGADATTA

28

Although we feel here at times like inhabitants of different realities thrown together, in that very discomfort there is much to see—a close examination of everything that constitutes feeling threatened or alone. Feeling as though I have to defend my world view, on which I think my life is based. Thinking I have to defend the existence of women's suffering, or of my own suffering, against those who would question it or fail to recognize it, terrified that I'll lose my life, or everything I value, if I let go. Being with these feelings, watching myself sometimes open, or else watching as I close down. Seeing the attachment to my view of reality, my picture of how the world is. Interesting, often painful work. But I'm finding real excitement in discovering how things can be worked with in such a diverse group.

I can get very defensive and feel very threatened when I'm faced with five men over the breakfast table asking me if my feelings about a possibly dangerous man aren't really just images, memories, and thoughts projected by an imaginary self. It gets very borderline, this kind of stuff.

Toni gives no validation whatsoever to the personality,

87

the self, nor to any attempt to maintain separation or emphasize differences. She wonders why my writing group in California is all women. She questions any kind of exclusiveness. I feel disconcerted by her questions. Getting together with others with whom I share certain formative experiences and social realities, such as groups of women, gay people, or disabled people, have been liberating and empowering experiences for me, and I feel they have helped produce positive changes in the social structure as well. This kind of getting together is especially healing if one is part of a social class that routinely gets reflected negatively in the cultural mirrors—on television, in the movies, in books—or, in many cases, not reflected at all. Disabled lesbians, for example, are invisible. We do not exist on television. Perhaps straight white men have no idea what it means *not* to have that.

Or maybe men have been wounded as a class as deeply as women have, just differently. Maybe feminism has abstracted from the whole gestalt only our own story. Can we learn about social oppression without placing blame, without creating an other, without wanting to be the Most Hurt, without getting locked into a fixed ideology? Can we stay open to listening?

It isn't easy. I have so much charge behind all of these identities. So much hurt and anger. I knew people who were murdered because they were gay. Lesbian friends of mine were driven off their land in the country by neo-Nazis, others lost their children in custody cases. I have to go through countless situations in everyday life that open the old wounds afresh.

I go to the park and two male dogs start mounting each other. The owners are yelling hysterically at their dogs to stop, beating them, and then apologetically explaining to the onlookers that the dogs are "confused." Like me.

I'm working at an employment agency years ago and there is one woman client I really like, and I try to get her jobs all the time and we have long heart-to-heart talks on the phone and then suddenly it comes out that she hates gays. She doesn't know I'm a lesbian. I never tell her.

I'm eating dinner with friends and their six-year-old child. "That arm of yours makes me sick," the child says. "It makes me lose my appetite."

My friend Mary and her husband are trying to adopt a baby, and they finally find a birth mother who is pregnant with a child she doesn't want to keep. "But," Mary says to me, "we haven't seen the sonogram yet. We won't take it if there's anything wrong. We don't want a Special Needs kid." Like me.

I am eating lunch at a small cafe and there is a couple at the table next to me, and he is explaining his spiritual path to her. He tells her all about karma, reincarnation, the progress of the soul. He tells her that she was good in her past lives, because she was born into a healthy body. But, he says, if you have a butchered arm or something like that, it means you were bad. You did something you're paying for now.

Cripple. Queer. Girl. It means I'm bad. I'm sick. I'm a sinner. I'm unappetizing, unnatural, better off dead. A freak. I can't walk into a room full of children without it being a potentially traumatic event. I am full of rage and grief, and the only way out is the most radical. But I cling to my pain. I hear myself telling the story of how much I've suffered over and over and over again, like an old broken record, and I sense there's something false as well as true about this litany of oppression. I feel so humiliated, so deeply embarrassed.

I don't always feel safe about going to that no-self level.

Sometimes this approach seems to reinforce the invalidation and denial of our perceptions that we were all met with to some degree as children, and that women and minorities continue to be met with all our lives. When our reality is not culturally verified and we are made invisible, or made out to be crazy, we internalize this and discount our own feelings and insights. It seems to take years and years of work to begin to take one's own perceptions seriously again.

On the other hand, being here I've had to see that all perceptions are open to questioning, that these various political and psychological "truths" we construct in the process of healing ourselves aren't real either. They are constructions designed to explain reality, but they are abstractions and so inevitably fall short of the whole. They have their usefulness, but to the extent that we mistake them for reality, believe in them as dogmas, and identify them as vital to our existence, we lose the ability to question them and move beyond them. We lose the ability to see accurately.

Mel once said something interesting in a meeting with me. He said that Zen practice is perhaps particularly challenging and difficult for people like blacks or gays who are working on finding their identity in a certain sense, or regaining it, because this practice is about having no identity at all.

Is there a way for the two realms to meet, wholeness and particularity?

Perhaps meaning is not a fixed thing, but rather something that is continuously unfolding. Maybe it is absolutely essential at one time to be part of a separate group of women writers or disabled lesbians, and equally essential at another time to be completely inclusive and refuse all labels and definitions of oneself. Perhaps the point isn't that only one of these apparent choices is correct.

Toni's work is like realizing that we're all put here in various bizarre costumes: black skin, white skin, amputations, old age, cerebral palsy, Down's syndrome. Some people get more bizarre costumes than others, but everyone gets one, without exception. And then no one really sees anyone else. We see the costume. We can't get past it. Some people never even realize they're at a costume party.

I experience myself as a regular person who happens to be wearing this strange costume without a right hand. (A friend of mine in California calls her German shepherd the one in the dog suit, and that's sort of how I feel, like the one in the amputee suit.) Sometimes I feel unseen. Often I even forget I'm in costume. Everyone I see around me has two hands, so there is no mirroring of my body image. I tend to picture myself—in my mind—as looking like all the other human beings I see. There's often a certain shock when I look in a mirror or see myself in a photograph and realize I don't have two hands.

When dogs or babies encounter my arm—the one that ends just below the elbow—they see it without ideas. To them, it is one more interesting shape to explore. There is nothing taboo or frightening or repulsive about it. Dogs never lose that direct perception, but babies do. By the time they're three years old, many children are afraid of my arm, repelled or upset by it. Conceptual thinking has set in. Once grown, we can't become babies again, and of course we can't become dogs. But it is possible to discover a way of seeing that illuminates all the concepts and judgments that are superimposed by thought and social conditioning onto the actual facts, a way of seeing that reveals the simple shape of what's actually here. Meditation is that kind of direct and immediate perception.

Living here, I see men's pain. I am learning that men do not feel seen either, that the cultural stereotypes hurt them too, that many of them feel more alone and more hurt than I will probably *ever* feel. I don't envy them. I am constantly having to give up my ideas. I see how frightened we all are, protecting our ideas, feeling misunderstood. All the various constructs that I've built my sanity on are being questioned, and in that process it seems that my very life is threatened. Sometimes I don't know anymore what's true or real.

And it's scary, not knowing, in a group of mostly men. It feels as though I'm putting down all my defenses and they're all still armed, like unilateral disarmament in enemy territory. But of course, they feel the same way, and if we don't begin somewhere to disarm ourselves, we will certainly blow ourselves up. It is the human condition in microcosm, and this work we are doing here is the work of world peace.

"Look, Paul," I said, "I need some of my defensive ideas. Why, if I were to walk down a city street late at night without ideas, freshly . . ." I'd get raped, I had meant to say, but instead I stopped dead in my tracks and just wondered about it.

"You don't know, do you?" he asks.

I am furious. How dare some man say that to me! And yet, he's right! It's true! I don't know what would happen. I think of Peace Pilgrim, a woman who *did* walk down the city streets freshly and who was never hurt, because—she says— she didn't buy into negative images about people, but rather saw the light in them.

Everything changes so quickly here . . . the sky, my opinions, the weather.

I wonder now about my desire to be in the company of others like myself. Springwater is a world in which I am not completely mirrored or met. I am alone here in a way that I was not alone in California. And maybe that aloneness is a great gift because it is a ground for learning. Because what *is* that need to find oneself confirmed, to share experiences? Isn't it vital, if human life is to survive, that we learn to communicate across all these apparent barriers? Such communication may only be possible if we can actually see—moment to moment—the thoughts that sustain and create these separations, including the powerful emotions and chemical reactions that get triggered.

The others may feel exactly the same loneliness that I feel. Everyone has different reasons why, but the basic experience feels like a common human problem. We feel separate. And that feeling of separation seems to be at the bottom line of our human misery. How much does the company of like-people mask this basic dis-ease of feeling incomplete?

In one of their dialogues, Krishnamurti and David Bohm talk about the need to stand alone. Krishnamurti says that to transform your conditioning you have to be psychologically alone. Identifying yourself with a group is a way of escaping your fear by identifying with what Bohm calls a false universal. In order to move away from separation, one must be free of this false universal.

Sitting up at the pond, which is frozen over now, I see Toni and Kyle walking through the snowy field hand in hand. They wave to me. Kyle is a tender, sweet man who seems utterly supportive of Toni's work and unhindered by male ego, or much of any other ego. They have a lovely friendship. Maybe he is the only real friend Toni has, in the sense of another person who shares her insightfulness and is not her student. Sometimes I think it must be very lonely to see the truth so clearly. It would separate one from so much of what passes for human relationship.

Toni is quite literally living in a foreign country. She was born and raised in Germany, and then being the teacher here and being an older woman and seeing as keenly as she does must be a very solitary thing at times, certainly no less lonely than being the only one-armed dyke.

It seems to be a vital part of what is going on here to look deeply into the separations we feel and create, and to find our way beyond them. That is part of what it means to live here in this tiny community in the middle of nowhere, in the dead of winter questioning everything.

29

"There's too much pain," I tell Toni. "I'm not sure I can stand it."

Rain is splattering on the roof, sputtering in the gutter, splashing, tapping—wet, delicate sounds—washing over everything. Toni and I are sitting at opposite ends of her living-room sofa, talking. It is late afternoon, already growing dark. There is the energy of listening together quietly, the vibration of that, the stillness, the sounds of the rain.

"It takes enormous patience," Toni says at last, "to see the sorrow. To be with it. To not move away. Or find easy comfort. To look. To see human history. Because it's not just one's personal pain that is contacted. It's humanity's pain, the universal sorrow of human beings."

The rain turning to snow now, the snow beginning to cover everything over.

"Can we touch that pure sorrow?" Toni asks. "Not wallowing in it or running away from it—but just touching it, understanding it in depth, without being crushed by it?"

Silence. The room growing darker. The clock ticking softly. My meeting time is almost up.

I stand in the north field at twilight, huge black clouds blowing in above me, so low over the ground that I almost have to duck. Four deer run right in front of me, very fast, and I smell them afterward in the night air.

30

I went to Chicago for Christmas. The plane coming in over the frozen lake, my mother's high-rise out the airplane window, the icy white city below. Sixty degrees below zero here with the wind chill. There is a rigor in it, a freshness and energy, that thrills me.

My father has been dead for almost a decade, and my mother has sold the house, left the suburbs, and moved downtown. She blossomed after Dad's death, began traveling all over the world, her lifelong dream, growing more and more resilient and beautiful with age. A broken hip last year has shortened her stride a bit, but she still insists on crossing Michigan Avenue against the light and engaging in a constant whirlwind of activities.

She embraces the winter of her life with a fierce pride, wearing wild purples, big beads, and huge, colorful hats, signing up to see the world, an intrepid explorer imagining herself in the company of Indonesian chiefs and Egyptian queens. My mother is going on a mountain bike trip across Bali this spring, and last year she went to the Yucatán, where she climbed the pyramids. I have a snapshot of her in a huge red hat coming back down on her bottom, one step at a time.

My mother, who brought me into this world, is nearly deaf, her hair is white and thin, she chokes on her food ("I'm doing my eighty-year-old drill," she says—gasping for breath), she shuffles when she walks, and one day death will take her "forcibly into the very heart of that which exists" (Teilhard de Chardin). In the meantime, she charges passionately forward.

My mother's apartment is a colorful array of mismatched furniture (antiques and Danish modern crowded into the same room), art objects and trinkets from all over the world, wall-to-wall paintings (my mother's sister and her husband were both painters, and so was I long ago), exquisite pottery, plants (one jade plant as old as I am), and chocolate bonbons.

My mother has friends of all ages, races, and classes, gay and straight, from every conceivable walk of life. She is fearless. She visits one friend who lives in a dangerous housing project, striding in alone where few white people would dare to tread even if accompanied by a SWAT team. My mother has worked for years with a group in Chicago that opposes police misconduct. She is infinitely generous, and seems to say *yes* to everything that comes to her. Her life is about giving, not about getting.

The woman who cleans my mother's apartment is black and not much younger than she is. Once, when Estella was burned out of her apartment on the South Side by arsonists, my mother took her in and they lived together for several months, like a cantankerous old couple. Estella is infuriated by my mother's vegetarian diet, her no-smoking policy, her desire to use ecologically safe cleaning products, and on several occasions the two of them have stopped speaking to each other.

Sometimes when I am in town we rent a car to go visit Aunt Winifred and Uncle Harold, and if we pass a homeless person on the streets, my mother is as likely as not to invite them into the car and instruct me to drive them wherever they need to go. Once, coming out of a store, we passed a bag lady whose bags had broken apart. My mother knelt down and set about helping the woman pick up her things. She doesn't walk by people in need, nor does she allow herself to be intimidated by fear.

There is immense suffering here in Chicago—pollution, poverty, materialism, vast injustices, and inhumanity, noise, brokenness, you see it all streaming by you. My mother embraces all of it, talks to her plants and to the old and the homeless on the streets. Good morning, she says, this is life. Taste it. She takes the hands of the street crazies in her own hands, those bony, shaking, arthritic, large-veined hands in which I was once held.

I saw an old friend, another recovered alcoholic, and we had a big altercation. The same fight we've been having for the last fifteen years over our different models of alcoholism, to which we are both attached.

Barbara sobered up on the traditional AA model, and I sobered up through a blend of feminism, radical therapy, transactional analysis, and gestalt. Two completely different conceptual grids. Two different ideologies. Barbara still labels herself an alcoholic. I do not think of myself now as an alcoholic at all. Even the ex-alcoholic or recovered alcoholic identity is one I've begun to question. I don't (and never did) buy the disease model, and Barbara does.

I don't feel as though I know anymore how freedom from addiction actually occurs, whether it's a choice we can make or an act of grace or what it is. I wanted to explore it with Barbara. But there was no space to explore. Everything was already mapped out, and our lives depended on the old maps, or so we thought.

What interests me most is how we both seem to feel that our lives hinge on our ideas, our models of recovery. When that's the case, then there's very little space for listening or growing. I see Barbara's attachment more easily than I see my own, of course. The belief that I'm right is so strong.

It seems important for all of us to learn to listen to one another's experiences, and also to listen inwardly—to see the thoughts that begin to run like reflexes when our beliefs are questioned—to feel the sensations that arise—the adrenaline, the narrowing down. Whenever I feel those chemicals going, it's a clue to pay attention. What am I defending? In my interaction with Barbara, I can feel chemicals churning inside me, and blood rushing around. I can *feel* that I am not open to her.

Openness won't come by an act of will. We can only begin where we actually are—by observing the narrowing down, the defenses, the resistance—just being with that, seeing it, finding out what it is. And in a way, that's the last thing we want to do. We *want* to be right.

A life without addictive substances, or practices, or thoughts, is scary as hell. That's where Toni seems to be pointing. Let's get rid of everything. *Everything.* And let's see what's left, and what happens then.

At night, the high-rise rocks in the wind. You can feel it moving. Everything sounds too grandiose, too big. Toni would say it's all just more thought, more ideas, more self-centered dreams, all this stuff about getting rid of everything.

Who told you to eliminate anything? Look at the void in front of your eyes. How can you produce it or elimi-nate it?

HUANG PO

I realize more and more that the things about Toni that I don't like, or don't agree with, are actually the very same things that I love and am most attracted to. I get upset at Toni's apparent dogmatism about her pathless path, for example, and yet what attracts me to her is her ability to strip everything away. Then when she does it, I get irritated. I want her to appreciate the beauty and rightness of everything.

Chicago is getting hard. Outside it is gray and rainy. Barbara called to cancel our date tomorrow night, because she feels she cannot deal with seeing me. That made me very sad. And then it made me wonder if I am a poisonous person. And then it made me angry, because of course I believe I am not. I feel self-righteous, convinced I'm right, Barbara is wrong. My understanding of addiction is superior to hers. My self-awareness is greater. The opposite thought is lurking in the background: Barbara is right, and I'm way off-base.

Sometimes there is just the listening. And then there is no problem.

It is my last night in Chicago. The weather has been warm (thirty-nine degrees) and bleak. It's hard to leave Mama. This morning we fought. Then we rented a car and drove out to the retirement home to visit Winifred and Harold.

Winifred is the aunt who had the psychotic breakdown when I was born with one arm. She is now completely in outer space, with some combination of Alzheimer's, old age, psychosis, and the "side effects" of a lifetime of electroshock and drug therapies. My uncle Harold, who once wanted to be an opera singer but became a salesman on the railroad instead, is now an old man in his eighties with a florid, jolly face and thin white hair. He sits by my aunt's bedside in the nursing-care facility all day long, and does all her laundry himself. Today he has on red suspenders.

Loyal and hardworking, Harold lives without the comfort of any religious beliefs or practices. He was once a Communist, but he turned long ago into a Republican, and now we disagree violently about almost everything. Or we think we do.

Winifred forgets that Dad is dead and can't remember what she just said. She reminds me of a Samuel Beckett character. "Way . . . *way* down there," she says, "I think that might be my legs. I'd like to move them but I have the feeling it wouldn't be good somehow if things were rearranged."

Always it is emotional to be with my aunt and uncle. They were the extended family of my childhood, and now they are tottering into old age, and sometimes I panic and realize that I am middle-aged and my friends are turning into grandparents and what have I accomplished? Nothing. I'm a childless, careerless failure living at an unauthorized meditation center in the middle of nowhere with a bunch of belching men who watch television. Cold terror fills my whole body.

And now I am home. Full moon. The smell of woodsmoke and moonlight. Snow. The silence of Springwater.

31

Toni is away. It's an "off-period," as we say. There's a rhythm here of alternating "on-periods," when Toni is in residence and retreats happen, and "off-periods" without Toni, and without retreats. When she's here, energy is high. You wander into the kitchen for a piece of bread and leave three hours later after a gripping discussion about self, form, Springwater without Toni, authority, or some such thing. There are volunteers and guests around, plus staff. Toni shows Krishnamurti videos in her apartment in the evenings and afterward there are long discussions. Weekend mornings there are talks or discussions open to the public followed by a lunch, and a handful of Rochester folks usually come out for part of the day.

Then the off-period arrives and is a kind of break from this intensity, a quieter, more solitary time. Usually only staff is here, and maybe an occasional long-term volunteer like myself. People take off on vacations, and it can get pretty empty.

I have grown close to Paul. I feel such tenderness toward him, and from him. It has dawned on me slowly how fine he is. You don't necessarily see it at first, because there's nothing flashy or glamorous about him.

Last night Paul and I were the only ones home, and we had a long talk in the kitchen. He wasn't trying to be sincere or modest or sensitive. He just was. He had tears in his eyes when he talked about putting his mother's dog to sleep after her death. I realized that he's more politically hip than I thought he was, too. His college major was Black Studies.

I'm growing closer to people on staff, and also to the people who come here for retreats. There are wonderful people who come here. A mailman from New Jersey, a woman who runs an organic farm in New Hampshire, someone who cares for abandoned and injured birds, a psychiatrist from New York City, a filmmaker from Los Angeles, an art teacher from Cleveland, an English professor from Iowa, an opera singer from Texas, a philosophy student from Norway, an emergency-room doctor from Philadelphia, a jazz musician from Chicago, an engineer from Rochester, a commercial-airline pilot from New York, a poet from Georgia.

The men on staff are all reserved and shy, unpretentious, quiet, unaffected. They don't reveal much, or say much.

Sharon, the only woman, is the same way. It takes a long time to get close to them. But slowly, I've been getting to know them. Talking with Felix, a wildlife biologist with a graduate degree from Cornell who loves to roam around in the woods. He has a quiet, dry wit. And Roger, who dropped out of college, told me recently about being in Vietnam. He was drafted. He showed me a wooden statue of a man that he'd brought back from Thailand or someplace, and it had a huge penis that popped out. He grinned from ear to ear when it popped out. Roger worked at an auto-body shop in Rochester after the war, and then he met Toni around the time she left the Zen center. Every morning I watch him feed the birds, this balding, bearlike man with his large hands. Roger can identify the songs of all the birds. I would never have known these men in California.

In the woods there are many deer, and deer beds scooped out of the snow, and tracks of all kinds of animals and birds. There is a wonderful wet smell, of moisture and decay and rebirth. The sky here is always moving. Late-afternoon wintry sun coming in and out of fast-moving clouds, making the ice and resin on the black bark of the trees glisten with light, turning the pine needles orange and red.

In a small bush that sits all by itself in the middle of the path that cuts diagonally through the upper field, I discover a nest with empty blue eggshells in it covered by old wet leaves. Small miracles.

In the woods, an abandoned wasps' nest hangs from a tree, slowly disintegrating.

My friends Esther and Elaine arrive from California for the February retreat. I feel the closeness and intimacy I have with them, and when they leave, I cry openly, uncontrollably. This is a loosening for me, because I almost never cry, and never in public, and never profusely. But here I am sobbing. Roger and Felix hold me in their arms. This is home now.

32

I hear the sad news from Nicaragua of the electoral defeat of the Sandinistas. Violeta Chamorro, the Contra candidate, won the election. Hard to hear it here where some take it as good news. I am in a seething rage. Only Paul seems to fully grasp the tragedy of what has happened. He says to me over breakfast, "I was so shocked, and then I realized what had happened. The Nicaraguan people surrendered. Bush told them if they elected Ortega the war and the embargo would go on, and the hell they've been living in, and if they chose Chamorro, there would be peace, and they surrendered."

But the evening news paints such a different picture. I don't know how to be involved and not be a terrorist, I really don't. Mostly these days I avoid the news completely, not wanting to know. The earth as we know it may well be terminally ill, and yet that need not be cause for despair and hopelessness, as working with any death reveals.

There is a woman from Nicaragua, Julietta, who comes to every retreat here at Springwater. She lives in Miami now. She supported the Sandinistas during the revolution, but her family were large landowners. Their land, according to Julietta, has been poorly managed by the Sandinistas since the revolution. Julietta went to school in the States and came back here after the revolution. While she is sympathetic to many of the aspirations of the revolution, she nevertheless supported Violeta Chamorro, the candidate of the Contras, in the recent elections. Now she will return to Nicaragua.

We have become good friends, Julietta and I. We liked each other instantly. She is a passionate, warmhearted, energetic, intelligent woman, roughly my age. Knowing her has been another instance in which I've had to give up cherished, long-held ideas. I thought all the Nicaraguans in Miami were *gusanos* ("worms"), as we used to call them—rich, coldhearted, greedy people like George Bush and Ronald Reagan, friends of the dictator Somoza, people who threw tomatoes and rotten eggs and rocks at us during demonstrations against Somoza in San Francisco, killers who assassinated people on our side. The Nicaraguans in Miami were not people I would want to speak to or befriend. And now there are a number of Cuban and Nicaraguan exiles coming here to Springwater from Miami for retreats and I discover that I like them. They may come from the upper classes, their political ideas may sometimes differ from mine, but they are not as different as I imagined. In fact, they are caring, concerned human beings.

It's eye-opening to come face-to-face with the realization of how close-minded I so easily become, how stuck on whatever positions I have adopted, how unwilling to question them. Because I support the revolutions in Cuba and Nicaragua, and have been so appalled by U.S. intervention and aggression in both countries, I latched on to certain opinions and beliefs, and I wasn't listening anymore, certainly not to anything that contradicted my ideas. I'm not saying I agree with all of Julietta's ideas now, only that I'm more open to *listening* to them, to hearing her perceptions and considering other viewpoints.

In some sense, maybe I was never listening before.

Why is meditation political work of the deepest kind? Because it allows us to begin to question our firmly held beliefs about the world, our images about other people, our ideas about ourselves.

Sometimes people say to me, but this is just a head trip. Yes, it is! That's exactly where the whole problem begins—in the mind. As David Bohm spells it out so lucidly, thought participates in reality without realizing that it is doing so. It imagines that it is a neutral observer of an independent, objective reality, that it is merely reporting the facts. It creates false divisions and false unities, and takes them to be real. It is defensive and resists evidence of its inaccuracy. It becomes habitual, even addicting. The world as we find it today is largely a creation of human thought. "The United States of America" is totally imaginary, and yet it has taken on an astonishing appearance of solidity and actuality, as if it really existed.

I am coming to see that true meditation is a crucial part of social-change work, perhaps the most radical part of all since it gets to the root of all the problems. I say this not in order to discourage activism of other sorts, but only to suggest the possibility that meditation, in and of itself, is action.

David Bohm seems to be the person whose work interests Toni most right now. A theoretical physicist who worked extensively with Krishnamurti, Bohm has explored the system of thought in great depth. He is currently interested in a process of dialogue whereby ongoing groups of people explore talking and listening together in an unstructured manner. The groups are leaderless and agendaless.

As they talk together, things begin to come up—what Bohm calls "assumptions of necessity" or "nonnegotiable assumptions." These assumptions are thoughts or ideas we believe in and are not open to questioning. If you think about it, you'll discover you have a lot of them. Consider, for example, your views about abortion, gay rights, Palestine/Israel, Nicaragua, the death penalty, addiction recovery, God. A different point of view from one's own may well feel life-threatening. The idea of the dialogue groups is that by talking together, these assumptions can be seen, questioned, and perhaps softened. The way thought functions can be illuminated, along with the connection between thought and emotion.

Bohm believes that individual insight is not enough, because the problem of thought is woven into the cultural fabric. He feels that working together in groups of unlike people is therefore of the utmost importance. In the group, the essential thing is to listen. "There is no pressure to agree or disagree. . . . We look at all the assumptions. I'm looking at your assumptions and my assumptions. They're all suspended. I'm not deciding they are right or wrong. Or, if I think I prefer mine, well, that's okay. But still I'm looking at the meaning of what you say."

Bohm speaks of people participating together in a common meaning that is constantly transforming in the process of dialogue. This sounds strangely like Springwater. The purpose is always free to change. No one is excluded. We will sit down here and talk with anyone about anything. Whatever people bring up, Toni takes it seriously and wants to go into it. Nothing seems fixed or permanent. Of course, we do at times defend things and get invested in or identified with our ideas and preferences, but that process is always being looked at and uncovered. What at first seemed to be an annoyingly inefficient and formless way of working now seems radically open-ended.

Inquiry can exist only if we are free from the idea that any one system, theory, or approach can explain reality completely. As David Bohm suggests, reality is never complete. "There is no final meaning," he says. "The true perception of one moment would not necessarily hold for the next." There must always be open listening without conclusions.

Thought tries endlessly to put things in order and find security. It takes a subtle attention to not land anywhere, in any system or representation.

33

Today they started major renovation on the kitchen here, which no one had forewarned me of, so at midday the kitchen had disappeared. A makeshift kitchen is now set up in the dining room, and it feels, as someone remarked over dinner, as though we're eating in our fallout shelter. A nice dose of upset and disruption, but oddly pleasing too, as disasters often are.

It snowed today, huge flakes, whirling in the wind like a

white cloth. And then it stopped and turned dark and melancholy, with a light, sleetish rain. I feel homesick and lost, and don't know where home is anymore. What seems to have shifted is that there's more ability to just *be* all of this, less desire to be rid of it, or that desire, when it comes, is visible as just another desire, not taken too seriously. Sometimes it's all *seen,* and that's all. No judgment, no taking it personally, no desire to be better, no division between "me" and some imagined state called enlightenment. The obsessions about who to become, what to do, where else to go, seem almost absent at times. And at other times, they all come flooding back.

They want to put a toxic-waste dump near here. That's the local news. Maybe Chamorro will be okay down there in Nicaragua. Who knows.

Before this last retreat, one of my mother's (and my) friends appeared to me in a dream. Brenda is a woman in her nineties, and in the dream she was a kind of archetypal crone, and we were together amidst many people, and she was talking to me but I was distracted and not listening too carefully.

Finally I said to her, "You mean, the trouble is that we're not really here, present, and attentive in the moment?"

And she said, "No, that wasn't what I was saying."

I asked her what was she saying, and she said, "We take it all so very *seriously,* life and death." *That* was our big mistake.

Clouds sweep silently across these huge skies full of weather. Snow falls and blows into my face. I inhale snow-flakes. The air is cold and sharp. Cattails are etched against the snowy, frozen pond. There is ice under my boots, cracking as I walk, layers of frozen leaves. Deer at twilight meeting me in the field, like strange masked gods they stare at me, and I stare back, until finally they leap away, their white tails flashing against the dark woods.

The next morning, when I wake up at dawn, the wind is fierce and the world outside is invisible. Then suddenly, dimly, I see little tornadoes of snow spiraling and racing across the fields, and then again, nothing.

Winter gives way slowly to spring. The robins re-appear. The first peepers begin their nocturnal chorus at the pond.

I need these heterosexual men, and they need me. Some vital exchange is going on. Felix took me to the beaver swamp this morning. We were bushwhacking through the woods, which were filled with mist. We saw the beaver houses, the chewed-off trees. We walked over ice, through brambles. Felix bends down and delicately turns back wet leaves with his fingers, exploring moss and wood on the stump of a fallen tree, and I feel this sudden desire to touch him that I haven't felt with a man in a long time.

We sat together in the hot tub later that night, steam rising off the water and the smell of chlorine. And afterward I sat by the open window in my room listening to the sounds of the night.

A huge blizzard comes, blanketing the earth in snow, just when spring seemed finally settled in to stay. So many of the issues that seemed important when I first got here seem inconsequential now. My conclusions seem less conclusive. My heart no longer races when Toni sits beside me, nor do I try to walk perfectly if she is behind me in the walking line during retreat. I still experience her, in some sense, as a teacher, but it seems less charged now. I see that the only difference between us is in thought. I imagine that Toni is the teacher and that I am the student, but it has no actual reality. I am focused less on the personalities of Toni or Krishnamurti, on picking them apart, finding flaws or contradictions, and more often my energy goes into the inquiry itself, the looking. There is more compassion for the personalities, for Toni and Krishnamurti as people like everyone else—no longer always needing them to be black or white.

I am sitting in the meditation room, and out the window I see this huge orange moon slide up out of the hills. So I put on my boots and rush outside, uphill, through the mud. The air is warm but there is still snow on the ground. There is the miraculous sound of running water and the smell of it. A thick slash of orange light shimmers in the pond. The huge snowperson that Felix and Roger built last week, half-melted away, looms in the moonlight. Sounds of birds and night animals, the Big Dipper bright in the sky.

Another retreat begins. The mental frescoes, one after another, passing through my head. What I'd really like is to lie in bed, relax completely, sleep and have sex and overeat and be surrounded by people kneeling in adoration. But since I see that never quite materializes the way I want it to, I've decided to settle for enlightenment instead.

"That sounds rather . . . drab!" Toni says, putting her hands on my knees and laughing and laughing.

Looking for the extraordinary, we miss the (much more extraordinary) ordinary world.

34

Do we need self-esteem? Toni says positive images are as unreliable as negative images. They may be nothing more than manipulative flattery, projection, or wishful thinking, and if we are vulnerable to praise and flattery, then we lap it up and look for more.

I was praised as a child. My parents told me that I was a creative, intelligent person. It was great, in a way—certainly better than being put down, ignored, or abused. But it created expectations—ideas and images of who I had to become. And that carried me away from the joy of being and doing.

I can remember how my mother used to give me a pail of water and a paintbrush and I'd "paint" the sidewalk for hours. I loved the feel of the strokes, the way the cement darkened under my brush. It didn't matter at all that my work would evaporate and disappear. I was doing it for the joy of doing it. But as I got older, I began to compare myself to great artists, to feel inadequate, to wonder if it was worth painting at all if I wasn't Leonardo da Vinci.

Toni tells the story of being on an airplane and seeing a little boy across the aisle building with blocks. He is completely absorbed in what he's doing. He builds and builds. Finally the structure tumbles. His mother reaches over and picks up the blocks for him and puts them back on his tray, and he begins again. The mother pays no attention to him except to pick up his blocks when they fall to the floor—she is busy with another child on the other side of her. Toni comments that the mother's noninterference is a great blessing to the boy, in contrast to how we frequently lavish praise on our children, thinking it's a good thing to do. We tell our children how great their block construction is, how talented they are, how they're going to be a great architect someday, so that pretty soon the child is filled with ideas about being or becoming something, and begins performing the task in order to get praised, rather than for the joy of doing it. How lucky this boy was, Toni says, that he was being left alone to play.

If we see through the negative images, and they dissolve in the seeing, then that's enough. We don't need to add positive ones. Because if we do, we're not listening anymore, we're creating a grid—albeit a "positive" grid as opposed to a negative one. Any grid is thought-constructed and conceptual, and always based on the past. What *are* we, really? If the negative thought is seen, and drops away, and we add nothing, then what are we? Something much more immense and wondrous, perhaps, than anything positive that thought could conjure up.

But we never pause long enough to find out. We rush around, ever busy, always avoiding what is. Maybe the ending of all of that effort and noise and becoming is the beginning of real creativity. I read in a book that every cubic centimeter of empty space contains more energy than the total energy of all the matter in the known universe. The implications of that seem astounding. Empty space—silence—is where the potency is.

In the upper field, I met Paul, and told him I wanted to join staff. So I made my formal application the next day and they accepted me, and now I'm officially on staff, no longer a volunteer. I do the same work as before, but I get paid a small stipend and have a few additional responsibilities. I made a commitment to stay for another year, until next spring.

In the pond afterward, I found a rainbow, and fast-moving clouds, and the memory of one of the first Zen talks I heard—Reb Anderson saying, The sound of the trucks passing in the street should say as much to you as my words. And I thought back then, How curious. Now there are just peepers, and hearing. Undivided listening. The emptiness of it all.

35

Coming into California by air in the late afternoon, the earth below bathed in golden light. I'm on vacation, staying at Berkeley Zen Center, my old home, in the apartment where I once lived, with Mike Harryman, my old roommate. Mike and I had some terrible quarrels when we lived together, but at the same time there was a strong attraction between us. He can be infuriatingly arrogant and rigid one moment, and luminously open the next, and maybe the same thing is true of me. Mike works in the district attorney's office, which I find upsetting because politically I have always favored the defense, and sometimes I suspect that he votes Republican. The apartment is lovely, his taste impeccable. I listen to Bach cello suites and delight in the sweet smells of incense and flowers. On the breakfast table in the morning Mike lights a tall white candle.

There is a woman in a wheelchair, a quadriplegic, who sits regularly at the Zen center now. I feel happy to see her there, because I was one of those who believed in the importance of ramping the zendo—the meditation building—and it's nice to have another disabled woman in there. Turns out she's a martial artist and a dancer. Her name is Anne.

Mel, with his bald head and his tufts of white hair sticking out from his large ears, looks radiant in afternoon dokusan (a private meeting between teacher and student in which questions about practice are taken up).

"Being here makes me want to stay and not go back to Springwater," I tell Mel. "But I've committed myself to another year there."

"Stay with your intention," he tells me. "Let everything arise around it and disappear again. You make your choice and then you stick with it, and in the process all kinds of things come up—fantasies of better, more alluring possibilities, the desire to run away, the whole show—and you stay with that, and *see* it. That's Zen. Otherwise, you just create a lot of confusion for yourself and everyone around you."

I tell Mel I want to start sewing my rakusu again, the small ordination robe that is a sign of commitment to the Zen path, kind of like a wedding ring maybe.

I get into a heated argument with Mike over whether crack addicts and black criminals are lazy, evil people who are *choosing* to be destructive, while Mike, with the same pain they have, is choosing to be constructive, or whether people act in

terrible, evil ways because they are in pain and have no awareness that they have any other choice. My own history informs
me that the latter is the truth. Mike sees it so differently. He
sounds like Uncle Harold, with whom I've had several explosive fights over issues such as this. But, of course, Mike and
Uncle Harold are just as innocently who they are, and just as
much in need of tenderness and acceptance, as the crack addicts
and criminals they judge so harshly. Mike's and Harold's his-
tories have informed them of a reality different from the one
I see.

"I was beaten up every day on my way home from school
by a gang of black boys," Mike says. "And now they've destroyed Los Angeles."

"Maybe they didn't have any alternatives—or weren't
able to see them if they did. And maybe it was the white boys
who destroyed Los Angeles."

"Bullshit. They made their choices."

I feel identified with the blacks in Los Angeles, and therefore condemned by Mike's views. He's saying (by logical extension) that I drank because I'm a jerk, while he—with the same
pain—has become a successful lawyer and Zen student. I see
the identification happening, the "me" feeling put down, not
seen, not understood correctly. I see the defensive reaction rise
up, the hurt, the anger. I feel my breathing, hear the wind, a
car horn honking. I see Mike's pain, the boy who was beaten
up every day, shaped by myriad forces into a man with views
like these. And the argument passes. I don't need to win it. It
has no substance. It is nothing more than Mike's old hurt
and conditioning crashing up against my old hurt and conditioning.

I go over to San Francisco to get a haircut. Walking down

Mission Street. It's deteriorated so much. The street is full of litter and garbage. A group of men are being handcuffed by the police. A homeless man sleeps on a pile of rags beside his shopping cart, which overflows with more rags. A derelict lies passed out on the pavement. Urine smell. Cheap hotels. Scorched-out faces. The city seems so lost.

And then my haircutter's lovely apartment only a few blocks away, on a small street overlooking the community gardens. I have known Jeff for years. I know much of the story of his life by now. Jeff is a gay man who was once a soldier in Vietnam. He went over there as a teenager to fight for democracy, and was guarding captured Viet Cong soldiers when he started talking to them and discovered he liked them. He began to question what the United States was doing. He ended up against the war. Jeff has lived and worked in this same tiny studio apartment for the last fifteen years. He doesn't own a car. He has a sliding fee scale for his haircuts, ranging from twelve to twenty dollars. He is always cheerful. I don't think he has any big ideas about living an enlightened life—he just does it. I've seen him at demonstrations over the years for peace and justice. He's always kind.

The man who'd had his hair cut ahead of me had AIDS and was obviously quite ill. It was probably his last haircut. He collapsed in the hallway of the apartment building as he was leaving, and Jeff carried him back into the apartment, laid him on his bed, and covered him up. And proceeded to cut my hair.

I have dinner with Frank, my friend the cook who came west to chop onions. We sit in my car afterward looking into each other's eyes without looking away. There is no script for this encounter. It is not a prelude to sexual intimacy. We are being together without language, without boundaries. I feel fear rush through my entire body. Frank's face is so alive. I don't know who he is anymore. Feeling control dropping away, layers of trying so hard to be something else, something other than this vulnerable, open, palpitating organism. All the effort to control this aliveness, conceal it, disguise it, appear different from how we really are, different from the bare trembling of this moment.

Frank is holding the end of my arm now in his hands, and I am terrified but his hands feel warm and I relax. Red light from a neon sign pulses on and off on his left cheek. We are one being, yet we feel so much fear and separation, and at the same time, so much love. Looking into Frank's eyes, I see that nothing is solid. Wind blows through the trees. Light sweeps across the cars. Sound in my cheekbones. My hand begins to sing. My arm is chanting.

36

Anne North, the quadriplegic at the Zen center, invites me to breakfast. She is a beautiful woman and turns out to be a lesbian. We talk about all the attitudes we get from other people about disability. People saying things to us like, "I don't think of you as disabled." We roll our eyes together and laugh.

She makes pottery. Wonderful asymmetrical forms full of dents and errors that are exquisite and sensual and somehow very erotic. The beauty is in the dents. I feel a deep rapport with her. So much is instantly understood between us, without words. She calls herself a cripple. I like that. Crippled is a negative word. To use it is a kind of aikido move, in which the oppressor's worst insult is taken on and worn with pride. It's a strategy whereby you go right into the feared thing (hag, hussy, witch, dyke, spinster, nigger, faggot, bitch, whatever) and you claim it. You claim it and you wear it, you look at it, you pronounce it, you taste it, you chew it, you digest it, and as you do all of that, it loses its sting. It becomes just an empty label.

Anne grew up in Idaho and was a mountain climber before she fell. She is a winsome, wise young woman in her late twenties with wild auburn hair that flies out from her head in tiny curls, and she has the glamorous face of a movie star. She does karate, and dances in her electric wheelchair. She is part of a professional dance company that tours the U.S. and Europe. Anne is doing the very thing you would think that a quadriplegic could not do: dancing. And she is succeeding. Anne lives alone, sits at the Zen center, makes these wonderful erotic pots, gardens and dries flowers, and zips around like the wind in her wheelchair.

"I wanted to be a dancer," she tells me. "I figured I couldn't. I mean, I'm a quadriplegic, right?" Her eyes sparkle over the edge of her teacup. "But then I figured, why not?"

It's a huge joy to be with her, to be understood.

"I *hate* being a fucking cripple!" she tells me as I am about to leave. Our eyes meet and we laugh wickedly.

37

Toni arrives for her annual California retreat, which my friend Frank and I are coordinating. Coordinating a retreat is interesting work. It's a balance between two worlds: the world of work (talking, doing, thinking) and the world of retreat (silence, pure being, and listening). You have to keep moving back and forth between these two dimensions. You come out of the sitting room after Toni's talk in the morning and you just want to be there in the stillness and let the talk unfold inside you, and instead someone hands you a note saying they're allergic to their bedding, the toilet is overflowing, they think they have Lyme disease, or they've just broken their ankle, and you have to deal with it.

Frank and I get into all kinds of power struggles. We have different ideas about how to coordinate. There's anger, irritation, and frustration, and one morning we have a huge tangle in whispers. I'm seeing my desire to control people, to punish them if they aren't behaving the way I think they should be. I'm terrified that everything is going to get out of control if I don't manage it. I walk into a room and see all these retreatants sprawled out on the couches asleep, mouths open, others reading books, one woman writing letters, and my mind reacts like a Calvinist minister. I want to shape these people up. But Toni just lets it all happen.

I see my compulsive speediness, my addiction to tasks.

"Slow down!" Toni says to me.

All of this is happening in the middle of retreat, so you keep coming back into the silence, hearing Toni's talks, working with all this material in a meditative way as a result. I am seeing that it isn't *my* stuff (that I need to feel guilty or ashamed about). It's our collective human stuff manifesting. Just to see it, without judgment, has its own action.

Coming home in the end after the retreat to Mike. His face is so open and unprotected. "It's all empty, all made up, we're just wind," he says. "If we really realized how much freedom we have, we'd freak out."

38

I have lunch the next day with a woman priest named Wayu who lives at the Zen center now. She has a shaved head and a striking, androgynous face. Wayu talks about allowing ourselves to *enjoy* the religious aspect of Zen, the ritual and form and beliefs. She feels this is connected to heart warmth and to art (ambiguity, mystery, adoration), that it taps into an intuitive quality that bypasses the rational mind. Liturgy is poetry; it cannot (and should not) be explained or understood.

"Erotic energy goes into the devotional," Wayu says.

I find this an intriguing thought, in fact, I find it an erotic thought. I feel slightly turned on. It brings to mind something Thomas Merton said once. He was talking about the joy of serving the Mass: "Saying the *pater noster* is like swimming in the heart of the sun." Ritual is a joyous love song to God, something to delight in and enjoy: deep fun. I am already imagining myself returning to California next spring, moving into the Zen center and becoming a priest, swimming in the heart of the sun.

Mike's electric shaver buzzes down the hall. Birds singing. I am drinking Morning Thunder tea. We get into a fight. He tells me I'm "needy," and "demanding," and "oppositional," and then refuses to talk about it. I feel unjustly accused. I *know* it isn't true. I can't believe he's going to say those things and then refuse to deal. I try to be "nice," placating him, soothing him. But I *feel* angry and hurt. I *am* needy. And demanding. And oppositional.

He won't deal. There's nowhere to go with it but inside.

I spend the day washing his windows, cleaning his altars, his bathroom, his rugs. Thinking about the times he's blasted his TV when I'm asleep. About the times he's lectured at me, setting himself up as my teacher. Thinking about the night he asked me to sleep with him. (I'd thought about it myself, but I said no.) Thinking about his refusal to see his part in all this. I am furious and self-righteous, and I spend the day building my case, compiling my points, my justifications, my grievances, judging him.

My friend Elaine wants to quarrel with me in the restaurant over dinner. I don't want to fight in public. I'm trying to soothe everything out again. Elaine says she can't trust me.

Being with all of this disturbance, seeing it, watching how thought operates, how the bodily sensations we call emotion follow, and then more thoughts.

And then that night Mike tells me how wonderful I am, and he has his lovely, luminous Buddha smile, and he hugs me. Everything is let go of. Nothing is held.

I saw Anne North dance the night before I left for Springwater. She was breathtaking, sailing around the stage in huge, graceful arcs. Lyrical.

> *Make me to hear joy and gladness; that the bones*
> *which Thou hast broken may rejoice.*
>
> FIFTY-FIRST PSALM

39

June retreat just over a few hours ago, light rain. I come to my room to be alone with my words, these silent prayer beads along which I feel my way in the darkness. Outside the sky turning a soft pink and then blue.

How was the retreat? Every time I got to the edge of enlightenment, a mosquito appeared without fail. Or a deerfly. Once, by the rim of the pond, I got so close (to enlightenment, not to the water), and then I heard it, that little whining sound in my ear.

I was the breakfast cook. The perfect job. Bliss. Up at three-thirty in the morning to cook. "The mouth of a monk is like an oven," I read somewhere. "In the night of our technological barbarism," Merton says, "monks must be as trees which exist silently in the dark and purify the air."

He also said that monks are "deliberately irrelevant."

Spring has come with a great overgrown passion. Abundance and lushness. Thunder crackles in the sky. Everything is moist and green, and tiny orange butterflies drink from the wildflowers that fill the fields. It is humid, almost tropical. Dark, fast patterns of wind race across the skin of the pond. At night, the fields are filled with fireflies, millions of them, blinking on and off like a miraculous light show.

I had the idea that Felix and I would become lovers when I returned from California. Our relationship seemed to be moving in that direction, we had even talked about it. But when I got back, I learned that he has gotten involved during my absence with a woman from Rochester, and now they are lovers. I feel disappointed, and maybe a little relieved. I sense that a relationship isn't really what I most want or need right now.

"Touch the sadness," Toni says. We so rarely do. We're so afraid of it. Thoughts come, and with them some ancient grief fills me up, and the fear of drowning in it and never resurfacing. I bite at one of my fingers.

I obsess over my imaginary choice between Zen and Toni, between Springwater and California. What to do next April. Where to go. Who to become. The familiar rut into which thought throws itself with such passion.

Sometimes I long for something besides attention: erotic devotion, mystical beauty—incense and Gregorian chants. I begin to imagine myself as a Catholic hermit. Someone tells me about a Catholic monastery in Colorado where women and men live together in the same monastic community as solitary contemplatives. It sounds perfect for me. I begin plotting my trip to Colorado.

I have always been attracted to Catholicism. Of course, I am appalled by the patriarchal Roman institution with its right-wing papacy, its obscene opulence, its narrow-minded morality, its condemnation of gay sexuality and birth control, its refusal to ordain women, and all the rest. Admittedly, it's a horrifying picture, about the worst I could possibly imagine. But there's something beyond all of that that attracts me to Catholicism, something that perhaps even *includes* all of that, so that one must find God not separate from, but in the midst of, the full spectrum of humanity with all its corruption, bigotry, and greed.

I am drawn by the garish crucifixes, the candles, the incantations, the primeval mystery of the Mass in its dark, sensual profundity—the whole polluted feast of life and death. Catholicism, like Hinduism, is a world where gaudiness and holiness intermingle inseparably—Kali wearing her necklace of skulls, the crucified Christ dripping blood, Hindus swooning and throwing flowers. Toni is more like a Unitarian and a scientist. She wanted the Zen chants to be in English back when she was teaching at the Zen center—so they could be "understood"—and then later she eliminated them altogether.

I tell Felix about my attraction to Catholic monasticism.

He looks puzzled. "Why would you want to give your energies to an institution like the Catholic Church?" he asks.

"Because there's a certain quality in Catholicism that appeals to me," I tell him. "A certain truth."

"What is it?" he asks.

"Something about love and heart," I explain. "Even their vow of obedience has some truth in it that I like, about letting go of my self-righteous attachment to all my ideas and beliefs."

"But why be a Catholic?" he persists. "Why not just have the love and the heart and the nonattachment?"

Indeed! Why not? Like some Zen book I read years ago: If you think you'd be happier with a new car, skip the car and just be happier. Or Mel's question to me in a long-ago dokusan: "Are you looking for something *real* or something substantial?" I told him I was still hoping to find the right substance, and we laughed and laughed at my delusion.

40

In zazen what you are doing is not for the sake of anything....
It is the activity which appeases your inmost desire.
But as long as you think you are practicing zazen
for the sake of something, that is not true practice.

SUZUKI ROSHI

A tiny spotted fawn runs up to me in the woods and presses its nose against my leg. The song of red-winged blackbirds fills the air. Bees bump into the window glass as I write. Despite whatever flaws may exist, there *is* a truth here, an openness and a simplicity that I value above all else. How could I even think of being a Zen priest or a Catholic nun? It's absurd.

Sometimes on retreat I wonder, How did we all get here? Toni, who walked out of Nazi Germany, cities on fire, to arrive here in this stillness. Frogs shrieking. White moths fluttering in the moonlight. Hailstones, huge ones, pelting the windowpanes now. It is almost completely dark outside.

I'm reading Rupert Sheldrake, a radical biologist who contends that natural patterns are more like habits than timeless laws. Sheldrake has this idea that when some members of a species learn something new, the ability of other members of the species to learn it should increase all over the world because of what he calls morphic resonance. Something like it was popularized a while back in a book I remember reading called *The Hundredth Monkey* by Ken Keyes. That book referred to a study of monkeys on some island. Once a critical number of monkeys learned a new behavior, then suddenly *all* the monkeys knew it, not only all the monkeys in that particular troop, but monkeys on other islands as well, where there was no direct contact. It was as if some field of consciousness was altered when the hundredth monkey caught on, and as soon as that happened, the information spread to everyone who was tuning into that field.

Such theories, if true, have interesting implications regarding meditation, and might suggest the relevance of meditation to larger issues of social change, since any one of us might be the hundredth meditator. If a critical mass of people wake up it could provoke a paradigm shift into a new way of being that is holistic, that understands the operation of thought and does not mistake it for reality. This would change the entire situation of the universe as a whole.

Of course, such a notion gives great energy and pleasure to a person who is meditating. Here at Springwater, any attempt to turn this open listening into something purposeful is seen and questioned. Radical subtraction, I have called this work. The dissolving of ideas until finally there is nothing but listening itself.

"Seeing how the human mind operates" can become a huge agenda, and perhaps a grandiose illusion. I have thought I was on the vanguard of human consciousness too many times in my life not to be suspicious when I find myself developing such a picture. I feel self-righteous and defensive about this meditation work at times, overcome with a kind of missionary fervor to convert people. This is obviously not open listening at all. The "me" is there at the center identifying with this "spiritual" project as I once identified with my political ideology. It becomes an extension of the self, a belief system, not a living process—and the belief becomes more important than real relationships or real listening. I have become suspicious of all such urgent missionary impulses to save the world. Who can say where we are going or what's supposed to happen? What colossal arrogance to imagine ourselves saving the world! But at the same time, who can turn away?

> *"Sooner or later the world must burn, and all things in it—all the books, the cloister together with the brothel. . . . Sooner or later it will all be consumed by fire and nobody will be left—for by that time the last man in the universe will have discovered the bomb capable of destroying the universe and will have been unable to resist the temptation to throw the thing and get it over with.*
> *"And here I sit writing a diary.*
> *"But love laughs at the end of the world . . ."*
>
> THOMAS MERTON

41

There was this thought today that I should return to Zen, and be ordained as a priest. It's a way of saying, Okay, I'll stay right here on this spot, I'll settle the self on the self, I won't move away, I'll stop dreaming and see what this is, right here. End of travel dreams. Vow of stability taken at last. But why wait for tomorrow to do that, somewhere else? Why not exactly here, right now—this moment?

All of this thought and fantasy is mind-spinning, endless postponement.

"Intelligent practice always deals with just one thing: the fear at the base of human existence, the fear that *I am not,*" Joko writes in her book *Everyday Zen*: "Fear takes the form of constantly thinking, speculating, analyzing, fantasizing. With all that activity we create a cloudy cover to keep ourselves safe in a make-believe practice."

Suzuki Roshi says, "There is no such time as 'this afternoon' or 'one o'clock' or 'two o'clock.' At one o'clock you will eat your lunch. To eat lunch is itself one o'clock. You will be somewhere, but that place cannot be separated from one o'clock. For someone who actually appreciates our life, they are the same. But when we become tired of our life we may say, 'I shouldn't have come to this place. It may have been much better to have gone to some other place for lunch. This place is not so good.' In your mind you create an idea of place separate from an actual time."

Talking to Paul in the gathering darkness, about Toni being hard to swallow because she offers nothing. We talk about self-deception, and wanting, wanting something from Toni, wanting her to be the teacher. A great, incredible wind sweeps through the trees, and afterward I walk up to the pond and watch the moon and the water and the darkness.

I dream I'm on the verge of renting an apartment I don't want in California. It's at the top of a flight of narrow, precarious stairs, especially difficult to navigate with one arm, for some reason. I realize the room isn't safe in earthquakes and that it doesn't have a good view—it's partial and obstructed.

Above the room, which is suddenly roofless, there is a trapeze that people are on, flying through empty space. This swing seems high and dangerous and terrifying to me. I don't want to go on it. It is attached to nothing.

42

I long for more discipline here. Less sloppiness. More silence. Sometimes I want to run away, literally, get on a plane and leave. The seeming disorganization and naïveté get to me, the way Toni asks everyone's opinion about everything and takes it all so seriously, the mass denial of what I perceive to be the Party Line, the heat, the ever-unfinished building, the way people seem not quite to connect some of the time, the lack of real intimacy and emotional openness of the kind I had with my friends in California.

Wayu once said to me that the difference between one monastery and another is nothing more than the difference between the dream you had last night and the one you had the night before. I am struck by a line from Dogen's *Genjokoan:* "To carry yourself forward and experience myriad things is delusion. That myriad things come forth and experience themselves is awakening."

It's like reaching for my pillow in the middle of the night. The hand that reaches for the pillow in the middle of the night speaks louder than words or stated intentions. The pillow I've reached for is Springwater, but my thoughts are filled up with everyplace else.

Delicate flower arrangements appear throughout the house. Felix gathers wild chanterelles in the woods and cooks them for our lunch. Orange newts emerge on the forest floor. I listen to a recording of Harry Belafonte at twilight with Paul. The listening is a kind of prayer, the voice pristine and exquisite, completely androgynous. I talk to Felix in the kitchen, late into the night. Everything feels quiet afterward.

Waking up in the early-morning silence, the wind blowing and the crows crying, feeling soft and happy to be alive. There is great love in the world, tremendous tenderness and grace, despite all the terror and greed and hatred. That we survive the pain and continue. Here we look at the roots of it all inside our own minds, and seeing that, I am truly amazed the world hasn't yet blown itself up. But here we are. Another day of life!

43

Hot does not begin to describe how hot I feel. I can't believe I'm still breathing. My glasses are steamed up. My hand sticks to the page as I write. And then suddenly, torrential rain pours out of the sky and we all rush about madly closing windows and mopping the floors. I am soaking wet. Lightning flashes in the sky and thunder crashes. Rain drenches the earth.

The cushions are coming out of the sitting room, although anyone who wants to use one can take one back in, but we no longer want to imply that cushions are in any way more official or correct than chairs. Toni has begun to suggest that other people here give talks and that we have group meetings as well as private meetings during retreats. Next year we will have a retreat with Toni as a participant. She won't give talks or hold meetings. There will be a sign-up sheet for anyone else who wants to give a talk, and a daily discussion group. The meeting room will be available for anyone who wants to meet with anyone, and there will be no timed sittings. And there will be two retreats a year without her.

❀

Columns of mist trail through the valley, the sky breaks open and a pale blue light spills out. There is a pinkish glow on the earth, turning into a deep red. The clouds are on fire, blowing silently across the pond.

We had a one-day sitting in the rain. All day listening to the wet, clean sounds. The delicacy of it. In the face of death, what is really important after all? Kindness. Love. Enjoying the sound of the rain.

44

I've been disturbed all week. It began when the Catholic hermits in Colorado sent me some tapes I'd ordered. I'd been having Catholic nun fantasies again. But when I listened to their tapes, it sounded to me as if they were pro-pope, pro-Ratzinger, antiabortion, antigay, antifeminist, and anti-premarital sex. I was filled with the pain of being hated and condemned because I am a lesbian, old pain from years ago when I started to drink.

So much for that dream. I certainly can't live in an antigay, antifeminist environment. One more phantasm shot to hell. Once again, stuck in the present tense, right here on the spot.

Toni says the whole movement toward a system, toward a path like Catholicism or Zen, is a movement away from the discomfort of all the loneliness, sadness, uncertainty, and incompleteness that thought creates, and from our fear of this utterly ungraspable, unknowable, uncontrollable spaciousness. The whole desire for a path is just desire to cover the pain with some form of fat, some anesthetization. It's an addiction, a delusion.

I see the truth of that in a more salient way than before. Yet I *want* it so much—a system, a path. Here at Springwater there's really "no thing, no body, no idea" to hold on to. "This is real poverty," Toni says. "Monastic poverty is just more riches."

There *is* something special happening here at Springwater. There's a different body-mind feeling, experientially, to working in this way, as opposed to doing some "practice," especially when I get clear about what's actually going on here. When that happens, there's a shift, and it's a crucial one. It has to do with completely effortless seeing rather than imposing something, however subtly. It's somatic as well as mental. I've been afraid of this shift, because when I *think* about it, it seems so empty. I want something to hang on to. So I've held on to Catholicism or Zen, as practices, as fantasy futures, as possible identities. But when I actually dare to lower myself down into this emptiness—no, that sounds entirely too dualistic and willful and "courageous"—but when this seeing suddenly happens and thought relaxes, Zen drops completely away, and something much deeper is contacted, some entirely other way of being.

The trick is not to make an idea or a system out of this openness, a new dogma. Truth can't be captured by thought or image. It can never be made into a program or a picture.

I talked during the Sunday-morning discussion about this whole experience I've been going through this week of listening to the antigay tapes from the Catholic hermits and everything that it's brought up for me. Looking at it together with everyone, I begin to see how quickly ideas and identities form around our experiences. The idea that I'm "a lesbian," for example. Actually, there's certain activity that occurs, and then from that experience and its historical repetition we draw a conclusion—an identity—and project a future: "I am lesbian," or "I am heterosexual." We identify with this image of ourselves, it becomes fixed, we see ourselves in opposition to others who are different and perhaps out to destroy us.

Sometimes I wonder, How can *anyone* call themselves a "heterosexual" or a "homosexual"? I mean, how can anyone *know* with certainty who they'll be attracted to next, what gender that person will be? Isn't it just that we *want* to be one way or the other, and we *have been* in the past, so we *think* we will be forever? Isn't it *all* completely imaginary, these supposedly firm identities based on so-called sexual preference? Not to mention the role played by thought, memory, imagination, and conditioning in determining who we find attractive! All of it is *so* insubstantial, so changeable. I've known many people who suddenly "became gay" or suddenly "went straight" midway through their lives. But people are terrified of not having a definite sexual identity. Our whole lifestyle gets built around a particular identity, and if we change, it upsets everything. So people love to believe it's all genetically determined and solid as stone.

In the tape from the Catholic hermits, I hear all the antigay attitudes and actions that have ever existed. I remember the gay people I knew who were killed because they were gay, my own pain as a teenager falling in love with a woman, my plunge into alcohol and drugs, and soon I'm defending my life and the lives of those I love and identify with. In some sense, this is real: Antigay attitudes (particularly in powerful social institutions like the Church and the government and the schools) *do* lead to acts that *do* kill people and that came close to killing me.

But in actual fact, my life was not threatened by hearing that tape. The feelings of hurt and anger and defensiveness made it more difficult to hear accurately what was said (undistorted by memories of what I've heard in the past), and this neurochemical smog, as Bohm calls it, makes it harder to respond intelligently. Is it possible to see that antigay attitudes are hurtful without interpreting them as the deliberate acts of a free agent, aimed at me personally? Hatred, bigotry, and prejudice don't come out of open listening and love, obviously. They come out of conditioning, fear, ignorance, and hurt. When we hear them spaciously, with interest and compassion rather than with hatred and blame, it breaks the cycle of violence, of attack and defend. It creates space for change. Because when someone thinks I'm an aggressive, mean-spirited jerk, I'm more likely to behave like one. We create each other.

The bottom-line nonnegotiable assumption, of course, is that I am a separate entity or personality who must be treated with respect, and who must continue to exist. Actually, as Bohm puts it, "everything is folded into everything." The universe is a holographic continuum in which each apparently distinct entity is a totality enfolded throughout all of space and time. Location does not exist because nothing is separate. A person is like a vortex in water—I appear distinct—but if you look carefully it is impossible to tell where water ends and vortex begins, or where Joan begins and the Catholic hermits end. The observer is the observed.

The sense I have of me as a separate entity is an image— a projection—and my tremendous concern with the continuity of that image is a by-product of thought and imagination. What Ultimate Reality has in mind—so to speak—is utterly unknowable, and in Ultimate Reality both Joan and the Catholic hermits are contained, as fleeting and chimerical as passing thoughts or bolts of lightning.

To see through the assumptions, to let go of them, including this most fundamental one on the bottom line, is total vulnerability. Crucifixion in Christian terms. You don't know what will come of it. You might die. You probably will. But the alternative, the old way, is nuclear holocaust.

So you risk something radical. And wake up. Suddenly there's no need to fight for anything. The fear is that we'll be back where we were before Gay Liberation—passive, in the closet, dead. But actually that isn't what happens at all.

We correct each other in a constantly evolving wholeness that requires all of us to be complete. To hear ideas that negate my image of who I am, or even my individual existence, maybe even terrible ideas full of intolerance and malevolence—to hear them spaciously, without resistance, without personalizing them—is this possible? It seems that it is, and that when it happens, it is an opening to a greater truth.

We are beyond all these opinions and categories that we identify with and defend to the death. In the sound of rain there's no separation anywhere, no need to keep existing, no possibility of not existing, no need anymore to become anything. It all drops away.

45

... in you is the presence that will be,
when all the stars are dead.

RAINER MARIA RILKE

Tonight there is a fierce rain. The sky electrical. The earth awash in water and wind. Tornado warnings. Brenda, my mother's friend who is in her nineties now, writes me of growing up in this part of the world, of terrible electrical storms, cows struck by lightning in the fields, and at night peeking out her bedroom window to see barns burning in the distance.

I've been corresponding with Anne North, the quadriplegic dancer from California. She's very young and exuberant and seems almost to idolize me, and it's quite flattering. She told me she has a crush on me, which I had suspected. I don't feel attracted to her that way at all, but I really do like her. I write back and tell her I don't want to be lovers, but I'd like to be friends.

There appears to be a shortage of staff looming, especially in the financial office, so they ask me if I'll start working in there, which means a commitment to staying here beyond next spring for another year, and I say yes without a moment's hesitation. When you see clearly, you know exactly what to do. My days in housekeeping are numbered and I will begin training in the financial office at the end of this month.

In the woods, I have crouched down to examine a dead chipmunk, her back ripped open, dark red heart exposed, eyeball popped out. As I stand up, deer scatter beside me. Light comes through the mist, dances on water and leaves. Winter is in the air, you can feel it coming.

I notice a change in my consciousness, maybe since I made this commitment to stay here, which has to do with the absence of thought about my future. There is more commitment to my life, not the *idea* of commitment, but actual presence in each moment. This makes me wonder if all the garbage really can drop away, not just for a moment here and there, but permanently, once and for all.

46

We're on a four-day experimental retreat without Toni: no timed sittings, no teacher giving talks and holding meetings. I'm writing and reading part of the time. I enjoy living with people in total silence, without eye contact or interaction, but with great attention and care. I like the feeling in the sitting room where people gently come and go in their own rhythms. I love the quiet. I enjoy being with nature, and with my writing at the same time as being on retreat. I like not having "Toni" around. There is absolutely no sense of a right way, no authority.

I was so opposed to having untimed sittings, it's funny. When this was first proposed, I feared the worst and fought against it. I thought it would be distracting having people coming and going randomly in the sitting room, and who'd want to sit in there alone if no one else came? The whole feeling of a serious retreat would be lost. It would be a chaotic, diluted, spineless affair.

But in reality, we seem to be one organic body moving with the utmost harmony. People come and go from the sitting room with great care, and on the few occasions when I've found myself in there alone, it's been interesting to observe the feelings, and in fact I enjoy being in there by myself when it happens. And miraculously, there are times when everyone shows up at once and there is a great shared quiet that is even more precious because it is completely unplanned, unrequired, unofficial, and unknown. There we all are.

The necessary work, meal preparation and so forth, happens smoothly (we do have job assignments and a schedule of mealtimes, but it's as uncomplicated as possible). It's quite lovely. People are truly quiet. They sit. They do what they do.

I want to go more and more in this direction. No more timed periods, no more Toni playing Toni. Let's just do this.

This morning, while we were swallowed up in an immense mist, Paul gave a talk, the first I've heard at Springwater that wasn't given by Toni. We had a sign-up sheet at this retreat for anyone who wanted to give a talk, and he signed up.

It was different from a Toni talk. Because Paul wasn't being set up as the Teacher. He was just taking some uninterrupted time to question and share with us out loud. He was wondering whether the way the mind sets "Toni" up as the "Teacher" is inevitable or if thought and imagination were creating this apparent problem out of thin air. He suggested that maybe one could hear her talks in exactly the same way I was hearing him, without the idea of Toni as the Teacher.

When Paul couldn't think of a suitable conclusion, he offered the sound of the pattering rain as his ending. It was sweet, and I felt a great tenderness for him.

This retreat was about finding my way beyond Toni. Beyond the ideas of myself as someone who needs Toni to see. There comes a point when you have to put aside all the authorities, all the dreams, and just be still and listen inwardly. It feels so scary, as if I won't be able to bear the aloneness, the uncertainty. The compulsion to reach for a book (or a teacher, or a lover) is enormous.

I suddenly have no desire anymore to train a new set of teachers to take over here when Toni dies, or to make myself into her successor. I am interested now in a whole new model of spiritual community, where no one is a teacher. Of course, this could pass. So many things have.

I've been bothered all this time by Toni's denial of her role, the apparent dishonesty of it, but suddenly I'm struck by the fact that I keep focusing my anger and criticism out onto Toni instead of simply not engaging in the whole thing.

Right now, like it or not, the fact is that Toni is central to our life and work here at Springwater. Without her we'd have no income, no money to pay our salaries or buy our food. I see how bleak and confused things can get around here during the "off-periods" when Toni is away (even the language we use suggests her centrality). I feel as though I'm in the midst of some kind of adolescent awakening.

"There's work to do," Felix said to me recently, "why all

this focus on Toni?" He's right, and essentially that's exactly what Toni herself keeps saying.

47

There is no bitterness like that of a man who finds out he has been believing in a ghost.

SALMAN RUSHDIE, *THE SATANIC VERSES*

The November retreat was all about rage. It was my job to time the sitting periods, so I had to be there in the sitting room. I was experiencing timed sittings as a kind of violence—having to "sit still" when my body obviously wants to move—and while that once seemed useful to endure, I am now wanting no more of it. It seems now as if it's about "me" trying so hard to Be a Good Girl and Do It Right and Improve Myself and turn into something other and better than what I actually am.

I didn't go to any of Toni's talks and attended only one meeting, and that one only to tell Toni I wasn't planning on coming anymore. We had a big dispute about whether or not there's authority inherent in the form here, whether she's a teacher or not. I spent the whole retreat furious at her, and furious about being a cripple.

All these feelings are surfacing about disability lately. I sit at the dinner table and wonder if my presence is repulsive to people. I feel that I should retract myself, disappear and become invisible, stop existing. And then anger because I have been made to feel this way, and more anger because people here seemingly won't acknowledge or confirm my pain.

A huge windstorm in the middle of one night. I thought the roof would be blown off. Trees were snapped off and uprooted. Some say the house was actually hit by a twister, but no one really knows.

The light has become oblique and far away. Winter is here. Snow and darkness and melancholia. The ground hard and frozen. Black crows flying through the cold sky.

Days in the financial office, making up a budget, which is like writing a novel. Numbers and words, so unlike the real world of housekeeping, where there are clean toilets and dirty ones, very straightforward. Addictive behavior running rampant: finger-biting, coffee-guzzling, thoughts about the future, even fantasies of drinking again. I experiment with not calling all of this addictive. Befriending it, listening to it. I remember Joko once telling me I am too absorbed in the project of self-improvement, trying much too hard to be perfect.

Not knowing what to do. A kind of yawning space that's a little bit frightening. No names for anything. No certainty. And under all this a seemingly bottomless sadness. Self-hatred, suicidal self-destructive layers of cellular pain. Little by little, over the passage of years, I lower myself cautiously down into it, facing it, discovering I can still breathe. Then panicking and brewing more coffee.

48

I've been talking on the phone a lot with Anne North. She's the only person in my life who understands how I feel. She confirms my pain and the righteousness of my anger, all of which she shares. Perhaps she also confirms my sense of victim-ization, my identity as an oppressed person, the idea of my self. Toni and Springwater allow for no indulgence in self-righteous or self-pitying stories about disability, gender, or anything else, however real they may be. I want sympathy and agreement and corrective action, and I want it now. I rage against the whole process of insight into the illusion of the self, which seems to mean that my life experiences and my pain are also illusions.

Anne, on the other hand, is all ears and all agreement. We bitch together, we laugh a lot, and gradually we become more and more flirtatious with each other. I call her up fre-quently. The first time I had breakfast at Anne's house, I was talking to my friend Esther afterward, and Esther said, It sounds as though you're in love. I said, No no, she has a lover. Then I found out she didn't. They had broken up. I felt panic. I'm not in love with her, I told Esther. I don't feel that way, I told Anne when she said she had a crush on me, and even if I did, I told her, it would never work. But then I was listening to her voice on the phone and suddenly I was swept away in something I didn't plan. Or did I?

I don't want to fall in love with a quadriplegic. I imagine us out in public together, a real freak show. Having normal lovers proves that I'm normal, too, so I like to have them look as good as possible. Of course, there is something intriguing and exciting about loving a quadriplegic. Where there's fear, there's energy. How would we make love? A one-armed woman and another paralyzed from the neck down. It is intriguing to imagine it. Anything might happen.

I am immensely drawn to all the work Anne's doing: the dancing, the artwork, the exploration of imperfection and limitation, and the limitless perfection of what is. I would paint her in motion, doing those huge swooping circles she does when she dances, racing through space in her wheelchair, soaring at high speeds, her auburn curls flying.

I wrote her a love letter, and in the postscript I said, "Don't think this means I want to be lovers." It was honest. I want to be madly in love with her, and at the same time I know I'm not. I am in the midst of some adolescent crisis with Toni, with all sorts of feelings and realizations about disability rising to the surface, having just had a disappointment in love (with Felix), while simultaneously undergoing this radical subtraction process here in this sometimes infuriating universe of heterosexual men who think differently from how I do. What better balm than to have a passionate love affair—at a safe distance—with someone who idolizes me?

I know all these things on some level, but I draw a curtain across my consciousness and pretend I don't. I feel genuine affection for Anne, but it's a fantasy person I'm in love with, not a real human being, not Anne North. We would not make good partners for a close, intimate relationship. Our connection is of a different kind. Some part of me knows that this is true, but I push it out of my mind. It has a momentum all its own, this dazzling, fiery falling in love.

49

The moon is almost full and yellow and the land is soft like a woman's body. The air is warm. The milkweed pods have opened and white clouds of seed are floating out over the fields in the blue light at dusk.

Toni came back last night and all my anger evaporated

because I love her. She is such a lovely soul, big woman who wears men's shoes because her feet are that big, dancing the waltz in the kitchen, alone, with all of us watching, around and around she sails so lightly and gracefully, with such tenderness and heart that I can hardly believe.

Anne wrote me a wonderful letter, responding to my love letter, and as I expected she is thrilled (or so she says) and anxious to dispel my doubts. We are falling in love by mail and over the phone long-distance. Sometimes she expresses doubts, and then it's my turn to come on strong. We take turns advancing and retreating.

It feels good to be wanted, to be seduced, to know I can charm someone. It feels enjoyable to be high on romance, to have sexual rushes throughout the body, to imagine making love, to flirt on the phone and in writing. Sometimes there are moments when I see what a sham it is, but the opening closes over quickly and I am again captivated by the fantasy.

Toni suggests in a meeting that these fantasies are a diversion, an escape from the fear of being nobody, from this aliveness that I am touching upon in this work. Maybe she's right, but I don't want to think so.

It is the night before retreat. I dream that Anne and I are together in the desert in an endless expanse of sand. The dream is rich with textures, surfaces, cheeks brushing together. Slowly, it becomes denser and hotter, more and more intoxicating. We begin kissing. I hear the wake-up bell. Four-thirty A.M.

Retreat begins. "Without awareness and clarity about

how this mind works, there is self-deception," Toni says. "Because thought will appear as real. Are wanting and fearing and the sense of separation from the whole inevitable?" she asks.

I feel an enormous wanting. Wanting Anne. Wanting not to want Anne. Wanting desirelessness and peace. Then wanting Anne again. I resist the desire, but I want to give in to it. There is a battle between two powerful self-images: the sober, chaste nun who is after enlightenment, and the bad, drunken "Real Me" who wants Anne.

Fantasies keep popping up. This is all imagination, I tell myself, a form of allurement. But I cling to it tenaciously. I feel drunk on thoughts. These thoughts about sex and romance are addictive and I feel a tremendous resistance to the threat of having them "taken away from me" by this work.

I sit with erotic fantasies in my mind hour after hour, watching and feeling them, my whole body electric with wanting. A state of total desire. I don't try to stop myself, but simply to see. I discover how addicted I am to ecstatic experience, to being loved.

I walk through the woods, delighting in my rapturous dreams until I notice what I'm doing. "Drop them," I tell myself. "I don't want to drop them," I reply, holding on. "It's delusion," I admonish myself sternly, "you had better let it go or you won't be clear." "I'd rather have my fantasies," I insist desperately. "Who wants a life of nothing but awareness? It sounds deadly, let's face it. Why can't you just let me relax and stop trying to get enlightened?" *"These are just thoughts,"* I yell at myself, *"Can't you see through them?"* "I don't want to," I reply, conjuring up Anne again. Habit battling with habit.

Whitetails leaping out of the sun-drenched morning field and the sudden smell of wet grass and wet earth all at once shock me awake. No more conflict or fabrication, no more desire for enlightenment or fear of renunciation, no more self-concern. Just white tails, wet smells, rolling farmland, a single hawk gliding through the early-morning sky. Nothing else.

What am I without my rhapsodies of Anne, or my obsessions about my future? Just this tremendous aliveness. The sound of wind. *This.* And the tremendous urge to get away from this.

Toni speaks about how the mind so often hears her talks in terms of black and white dualities or injunctions. Thought instantly translates what is said into good and bad, should and shouldn't, and then spews out new commands like "Don't feel desire" or "Pay attention" or "Don't think" or "Thou shalt be aware." But this isn't what Toni is actually saying.

She is wondering if we can listen to what we call disturbance without judging, resisting, or trying to change it. Seeing what happens to perception when thought is active, how emotions arise from thoughts, how anger wells up if I start thinking about what so-and-so did to me, or how grief comes if I start thinking about someone I have lost. If the commandment to "Stop Thinking and Be Aware" comes up—in a German accent, perhaps—can we hear it without becoming caught up in it? And notice the reaction to it if there is one? And not buy into the whole production?

Days pass one after another. Huge brooding clouds roll like mammoth caravans across the dark sky. Disturbances come and go, and Toni speaks of fine-tuning the disturbance, listening to it.

Your sole concern should be, as thought succeeds thought, to avoid clinging to any of them.

HUANG PO

I see how a moment of awakening is obscured by following some thought that comes up: "I want this state permanently," or "I want more than this" (I want Anne, too) or "I could have been awake sooner, but I blew it." Always the thought has to do with time, division, the sense of a self who is "having" these experiences.

In reality there is just endless weather. The pictures in the pond always moving. At night the full moon lapped by watery mirrorings of that fiery holocaust burning in the darkness—the sun on the other side of the world.

50

It turns out that I am no longer needed to take over the financial office. I'm back to housecleaning, which means I'm no longer committed to staying here beyond next April, which is a relief in a way, because Toni and I are having a hard time again, and I'm not sure I belong here anymore. I'm full of all kinds of primitive emotions. I go on day after day, irascible, melodramatic, offensive, and offended, firing off angry letters to one friend after another, imagining myself elsewhere.

"Why are you holding on to this identity as a disabled woman?" Sharon asked me. I was furious.

Deer-hunting/shotgun season is on, and the woods are a war zone. I'm on my third day of caffeine withdrawal. My body aches all over and I feel so tired it's unbelievable. But the headache is finally subsiding, which is a plus.

"Why do we continue grieving a loss for a long time," Toni wonders, "wallowing in the image and story of ourselves as a sufferer? And why do we bristle inside when this is questioned, instantly thinking it's a cold-hearted question?"

Death is something to be with day in and day out, Krishnamurti said in one of his books. How hard it is for me to part with a box of old keepsakes that I store in the attic, or to walk through a forest and let go of each precious moment as it passes. No wonder death seems so frightening, the thought of impermanence, the thought that there is no solid, enduring, coherent self, nor, for that matter, any solid, enduring, or coherent objective world. Everything is passing away, second by second. The *thought* of this is scary, but *seeing* it, when it happens, is creative and freeing.

There's such a world of difference between thinking and seeing. Mental concepts (such as "All is one" or "Everything is impermanent") can be used to justify behavior, frighten or narcotize ourselves. But realization, actually *seeing* those realities, is something else.

I wake up to a dark and stormy morning. The only sounds are the immense waves of wind and the occasional cry of a bird. The wind grows ever more rapacious, my room darker. I notice myself coming back into my body again. Caffeine puts me into my head and gets me going very fast, spinning my wheels much of the time in fear-based obsession, and when I stop doing it, I feel myself reenter my body and slow down again. It feels good. I am unfolding. I sit in my room doing nothing at all. Just being there. Listening, seeing, being. It's so scary to just be here, and then so wonderful, so effortless.

I think of Anne telling me to come home and be with her and how the words rushed through my heart. I imagine us

living together, a happy couple. Paul had tears in his eyes
when I told him I might go forever in the spring.

51

Everything shifted on this retreat. I went to every sitting, and
every meeting with Toni. Our connection was close. I went
right down to the bottom line, to how hurt I feel, the fear of
freedom, the fear of losing my identity—wanting to be the
one who has suffered the most, or the one who is most enlightened, and the defensiveness and anger I feel when something
shows me it isn't true, or I might be wrong.

Toni has her limitations, maybe, but she pushes on the
edge of things like no one else I've ever met. She makes me
uncomfortable, defensive, angry. I feel that it will be either
total salvation or ruination. I want to jump off the edge and
I'm terrified. And Toni just keeps saying, "Jump."

It really does feel that my koan here has always been
to be able to be here in spite of the things I don't agree
with without closing down or becoming defensive, angry, obsessed, and all the rest. "One should not expect to avoid bad
smells," Wayu wrote recently. "They teach well too." And
they do. So I'm still here, in this extraordinary place where
the deer are being shot, where people gather out of some in-
articulate love of silence to be together quietly, listening, wondering.

I called Anne after the retreat ended and told her I
wanted to stop escalating this erotic-romantic fancy. She
agreed, and we are conscientiously not doing it anymore. I feel
deflated, as if the air were being let out of a balloon. Not
acting on the impulse to do something is a way of revealing

the meaning behind it. David Bohm says, "True spontaneity may be the suspension of what appears to be spontaneity, but is not truly. . . . There are all sorts of clever ways in which the programs conceal themselves as the nonprogram."

I walk up to the pond and I sit there alone feeling sad, because the fantasies of Anne are gone and there is just the smell of dirt, wet earth, skunk, wildflowers, wet tree bark, old feathers, leaves . . . trees creaking in the wind. And thought says, This is not enough, this is too ordinary, something is missing. Thought says, I *feel* sad, therefore I *am* sad. And then in an instant the whole construction is seen as thought-produced. It's only there if I think about it, and in that seeing the feeling disappears.

But then Uncle Harold writes me a letter that seems to be telling me in great detail what a total failure I am, which he has done before, and although I tell myself these are all just thoughts and attachment to self-image, the self-righteous anger doesn't go away at all. Days of anger and hatred, the fear that he's right—I really am a failure, the need to prove him wrong, composing replies in my head and on my computer, cutting him to shreds, terminating our relationship forever. On and on and on and on. So much for enlightenment.

What was different about the two situations, the one where my sadness dropped away, and the other where my anger and hurt did not? Krishnamurti says, "If thought doesn't give continuity to feeling, feeling dies very quickly."

That takes awareness. If we *want* thought to die quickly we get into trouble. We can mechanically repeat the ideology of insight to ourselves like an incantation, hoping for clarity, telling ourselves, "This is just thought" or whatever, but unless the whole of it is seen instantaneously—including the observer

151

who wants to have an insight—then nothing changes. As Krishnamurti puts it, "Any movement on the part of the observer, if he has not realized that the observer is the observed, creates only another series of images and again he is caught in them."

How complete, whole, undivided seeing comes about is a mystery. Any formulation or method we invent will eventually get in our way. It's as if everything we learn must be instantly left behind.

52

The self . . . is a linguistic structure. . . . It lives via communication or dialogue, it is constructed of units of meaning. . . . It is a story; it is a text. . . . [Therapy] is a process of assuming or reassuming the authorship or responsibility for your own life text, your own self.

KEN WILBER

Anne says we must find the self before we can lose it. Toni says you don't have to find the self, because what is it? It's nothing but thought. Who is there to find it and what would they find? Does the fact that the self is a text, a construction of imagination, memory, and thought, does that necessarily mean that finding it (or writing it) is unnecessary or useless? Whether it is "necessary" or not, it is happening.

When we *think* about ourselves or other people, we appear solid and separate, our "selves" seem continuous, and there does *appear* to be psychological development. I was a drunk and now I'm sober. It seems that there has been an evolutionary process of some kind, an increase in awareness over the course of time. It requires thought, memory, and conceptualization to imagine this whole picture, of course. Me-now and me-then exist only in thought. They are images. To imagine myself getting better in time is imagination. That can be seen. The past exists only in thought and memory, and that thought and memory is always occurring right now as a present event. Everything is right here and now.

> *Each grass and each form itself is the entire earth. . . .*
> *Each moment is all being, is the entire world. Reflect*
> *now whether any being or any world is left out of the*
> *present moment.*
>
> DOGEN

Our seemingly separate "selves" are permeable, inter-woven fields of energy. And at a subtler level, there is only space. The text and the characters are imaginary. But I sense that in order to realize that fully and work on the radical level at which Toni works, one must have a certain discernment and a certain wholeness. One must be aware of one's feelings. One must have some sense of responsibility, empowerment, indi-viduality. One must already have a sense of oneself as a person with boundaries before one can begin to dissolve those bound-aries, because the point isn't to end up in a state of mind where you literally can't remember your name or set limits for yourself or say no.

I doubt if one could be in the state I was in back in 1973 when I sobered up, and work in the way that Toni does. I suspect that it was absolutely crucial that I explored my identity as a woman, a lesbian, and a disabled person before I got to Toni and started unraveling all of that. I was able to learn about my conditioning in a way that I don't think meditation, in and of itself, would ever have revealed. And Toni's emphasis on wholeness and nonseparation might have served to obscure and silence my own perceptions and experiences further. It might have colluded with the way psychological material gets repressed and oppression gets internalized. I've seen how people can use a subtly distorted version of meditation to keep the lid on and not deal with certain interpersonal or relational issues.

More therapists come to retreats with Toni than people in any other occupation, as far as I can tell. Many of my friends back in California are therapists. A number of spiritual teachers in the West are simultaneously practicing psychotherapy. Therapy literally saved my life. I think it's a great complement to meditative work. Without it, many people never really *see* the conditioned, reflexive, personal stuff lucidly enough to get beyond it, and it's that stuff (which *is* what we experience as "me") that obfuscates the realization of truth. But at some point, the whole psychological picture must be seen through. Any approach that sustains and strengthens the fiction (and the drama) of a self who improves (or declines) over time is ultimately an obstacle to fully realizing the truth.

Some teachers stress realization of absolute truth, others work more concretely with the relative errors in human thought that get in the way. Teachers like Nisargadatta and Krishnamurti give no foothold to the person whatsoever. They speak always from the absolute perspective. In awareness, when all the constructions unravel, there is no person who suffers.

There is *nothing.* That is the most radical truth. If it is *realized,* there is no problem. But if one merely *thinks* that one has realized it, then it may provide a rationale for dishonesty and disengagement.

Toni, like Joko, strikes a balance somewhere between working psychologically and working from awareness of the absolute. Certainly both Joko and Toni realize absolute truth, but neither one wants some *idea* of that to be used as a cop-out or escape mechanism. Sometimes in my own experience, when thought is running rampant and not being seen through, when things appear confused in my life, and there's a lot of chemistry behind it and messy circumstances, then the absolute approach may not make sense. I am more likely to pick up a book by Joko Beck than one by Nisargadatta at that point.

As with any living thing, insight cannot be forced or willed to happen, but it can certainly be cultivated and encouraged, as a garden can be. Toni questions the staleness and directedness of any method, and points relentlessly to *this* moment, which is alive and new and needs nothing, when we don't think we already know it. I love this freshness and freedom in Toni's work, and at the same time, I have found it tremendously helpful to sit quietly on a daily basis, to do retreats, to work with good teachers, to do therapy and bodywork. Toni herself is running a retreat center and teaching, so she obviously sees some value in those activities and forms. So-called practices may be artificial, but so is the way we habitually live, and rote attempts to put aside all methods, without understanding what that really means, may only leave us with other, unseen, conditioning. When there is not awareness, we are inevitably practicing something, whether it's meditation or old habits. In awakening, practice is no longer practice. It is effortless, choiceless, free. There is no more duality, no "me" doing "it." How that realization can be encouraged is an open question.

My experience is that different styles of teaching and different personalities of teachers are helpful at different times. There is a tendency to want to determine which version is "correct" or "best" or "most advanced" or "most true." But this is a mental game. The same tape, or the same book, can appear differently and have a different impact on the same person at two different moments. (Perhaps because there are only the *appearances* of "the same person" or "the same book," and in actuality no such things.)

Do we need to give careful attention to the text we call the self before it can become transparent? Is therapy, or any work that engages closely with the text, compatible with direct understanding that there is no self, that our personal history is imaginary? The answer for one moment may not be the answer for the next moment. It's a challenge to be with the question openly, because many of us are invested in our ideas (pro-therapy, antitherapy, pro-method, antimethod), so that we already have the conclusion, and we're identified with that conclusion—our livelihood or sense of self-worth may even depend on it, or we may *think* that it does. And therefore, we can't look.

And perhaps real looking has nothing whatsoever to do with coming up with an answer. "Yes, we need the self." "No, we don't." "Therapy is good." "No, it's a hoax." "All practices are obstacles." "No, we have to practice." Perhaps real looking or listening is something much more inconclusive and subtle and vulnerable. As Toni asks, "In the midst of everything can there be simple awareness, not knowing any answer?"

53

I just read a moving article about the life and death of Issan Dorsey, the gay priest from San Francisco who recently died of AIDS. Issan started a Zen center in the Castro district, and a hospice. We shared a similar trajectory through alcohol and drugs and the gay underworld, on into meditation. But Issan's history was even wilder than mine. He had been a female impersonator and a prostitute, had worked for the Mafia and been in prison, before coming to Zen.

I felt great affection for Issan, although I didn't know him well, but his openly gay presence at the San Francisco Zen Center in my early days there meant so much to me. I loved his humor and his lightness. He moved through the functions of being a Zen priest as if he were in a drag show. He took Zen seriously, but not somberly. He was always funny and always profound.

I delight in reading that at his funeral there was a photograph of him on the altar as a drag queen wearing a long gown and high heels and holding a champagne glass, and that Cosmic Lady, a well-known Bay Area street person whom I know, spoke at his funeral. I remember how tender and down-to-earth Issan was with the street crazies who wandered into the Zen center. He wasn't afraid of them or repulsed by them. He didn't think he was above them. He treated them like full human beings.

The last time I saw Issan was at Green Gulch Zen Farm the morning he told everyone he had AIDS. I remember he said, "AIDS is not the wrath of God; AIDS *is* God."

54

The snow is falling quietly this morning, miraculously, absorbing all sound. Crows sail on the snowy wind and Roger in his overcoat is shoveling off the decks.

Whatever is going on between me and Anne, it doesn't seem to go away. It blooms again, this strange attraction, despite my intentions, and grows larger every day. Suddenly I love it that Anne is a quadriplegic. Being a quadriplegic is part of her magic, her dance. I love her not *in spite* of the fact that she's a quadriplegic, but (at least in part) *because* of it. I feel happy when people see and love me as who I am. I feel hurt when they do the opposite, when they say things like "I don't think of you as having one arm." Falling in love with Anne is leaping into taboo material of every kind, breaking down conditioning. It creates possibility. It takes away limits.

I wonder if the desire for sex ever comes out of silence, out of real love. Or if it is always the result of thought, imagination, mechanical reflexes. Are we always just using one another, trying to fill a hole with a hole? Many spiritual masters lose all interest in sex (while others grow obsessed with it).

It seems that in the desire for sexual engagement there is an urge to connect deeply, to go to the bottom of everything, below the level of words and social veneer, to the realm of smell, taste, touch, animal sensation. And beyond that, to enter into a kind of meditative process—an uncovering—that can only occur in the mirror of relationship. It seems that a truly intimate relationship entails going through feelings of hatred, hopelessness, and otherness again and again, going through them and learning that they can pass.

There are great similarities between what I got from drinking and what I want—and get—from erotic encounters: a sense of complete surrender and letting go, of feeling absolutely powerful and utterly powerless at the same moment, in the best sense of both words, tremendously alive and totally relaxed. No longer judged. All inhibitions gone, all masks taken off. And there are great similarities in the depth of illusion and self-deception that is possible also, in the dependency on a substance or an object. It is dangerous turf, the erotic. Dangerous and also fertile.

To fall in love is to be willing to be out of control, foolish, completely vulnerable. Erotic energy is a fire into which my whole being is ready to plunge and burn. Suddenly I'm charging full-force after a vision. I'm not listening anymore. This is a free fall, part creative and part ancient habit. But who can say, really, what forces are behind it. It is an electrical storm. It's happening.

55

I am beginning to see how pervasive shame is, a thought that whatever I just did or said or felt is not okay (sometimes a memory of something I said or did ten or twenty years ago that's not okay), and immediately another thought that I am fundamentally not okay as a person. I'm so insensitive, stupid, coldhearted, I don't even deserve to live. And a bodily feeling of creepiness.

I can binge on these thoughts, spend hours in complete

self-hatred, thinking of one incident after another in which I said or did something I now regret. And then obsessive, addictive finger-biting, in which I cannot do anything except sit frozen in fear and self-hatred.

It's a shift that I'm *seeing* this, and beginning to see that these are *just thoughts* and the accompanying physical sensations, all of it arising automatically out of conditioning. I think for my whole life this has been going on without awareness—and I have believed it completely, taken it as truth, lived out of it. It's painful to see. To be conscious of all this pain.

We are on the brink of all-out war in the Middle East. I see pictures in the newspaper of small Arab children carrying gas masks, trying to look brave.

Whispering to Anne on the phone long-distance late at night, the night before I leave for Chicago. The radio station that the telephone picks up is broadcasting about the impending war simultaneously. And in the morning a huge wind is howling, roaring, crashing over the land. Roger drives me to the airport and we see an old workhorse alone in a field at dawn scratching herself on a tree, and Roger smiles, a big, broad smile.

56

Home to Chicago where everything is concrete except the lake, which is very organic. There is the grotesque fanfare of Christmas on Michigan Avenue, consumerism gone mad, women in furs, ornaments that must have cost a fortune. There is my mother growing old, and Anne on the phone. And down in the underground pedestrian tunnel that goes under the Outer Drive, down there in the dank, piss-smelling darkness, a homeless person has constructed a makeshift living room with cardboard walls, and a kind of bed, and a table with two overflowing ashtrays on it.

I saw an intriguing exhibit of the works of ten contemporary Japanese sculptors. It was an appreciation of impermanence, decay, brokenness, poverty. One huge fanlike object made of pieces of wood had a form in it that was so sensual, so curving and graceful, that I went up to look closely, and it was an old rotting phone book.

"I don't care if a work of mine is destroyed by the wind or rots in the rain," one of the artists said.

The concept of completion is antithetical to their vision. The parallels between materials that are breaking down and bodies that are breaking down is striking to me. The beauty of imperfection and decay. The physicality of it attracts me, and the temporariness.

I walk through the huge charred sculptures, the parasitical pieces multiplying and growing out of the wall, and my body is on fire with Anne, her words hang in my mind, and I am drawn toward her, into the darkness, into the primitive heart of all creation. "This longing, so intense, so deep, so ancient as to be the primal root of all the *is*-ness that *is*," she writes in one of her letters.

We became lovers over the telephone in the middle of the night. It was a strange way to begin a relationship, in separate time zones. But it happened. I'm going to see her at the end of January. And then in the springtime I imagine that

I will return to California and live with her. I tell my mother that I am in love. I tell everyone that I am in love.

My mother and I celebrate the New Year together, and then I am back again in Springwater where it is snowing and silent. It is the dead of winter. The cascade is iced over completely, the fields are frozen like diamonds, everything is stripped bare. Crystalline, compact, no extras. Stark and astonishing. The air is as clear as it can be and my heart is full of Anne. The fragility and vulnerability of life is suddenly extremely apparent. And the world is poised on the brink of war.

57

The bombing of Baghdad has begun. Roger came to my room and wept on my shoulder.

I called Anne and realized that the war will have an effect on my visit to California. Our whole mood is shifted by it, and Anne is running herself ragged with protesting. I resent the war for disrupting my love life. Desert Storm is not the backdrop I wanted. This is an obscene thought under the circumstances, but it appears again and again like a gigantic, hungry mosquito.

Two desperate men, Bush and Hussein—neither will back down. After the war broke out, I became addicted to the television news, Desert Storm in progress, blow by blow. We've been at war all my life and throughout the whole of human history, and in some way we love our dramas, our terrible stories culminating in death. We pretend we don't, but we produce them over and over again, fascinated in some way with the horror. We rush off to battle, for or against, hating Hussein or hating Bush, and the war is inside us, the seed of the war, and we never notice.

We want the black-and-white picture, someone to blame. So we blame George Bush or Saddam Hussein, or black people or white people, or capitalism or communism, or the left or the right, or human nature, but reality is something else altogether. I could be any of those people. None of their behavior is anything I haven't—on some scale—done myself. If you see that, and any real meditation work will reveal it to you beyond the shadow of a doubt, then you cannot possibly imagine that there is a "solution" to be found in fixing blame.

Retreat comes in the midst of this like an old and welcome friend. It feels like the end of the world. And yet so much possibility, so much tenderness is going on too. Toni looks full of wonder, and tells me that the hymn "Amazing Grace" was written by a slave trader who saw the light one night at sea.

I will miss this place when I leave and return to California. The affection I feel for each object, each jar on the kitchen shelves, the stove, the hallway, the door to my room, it all resonates. The silence of the sitting room late at night or before dawn in the barest part of winter, when it is below zero outside.

My criticisms of Toni are insubstantial and meaningless, nothing but envy turned into tearing her down. I see that. Toni is decent and sincere, not flawless, but vulnerable and awake. This place is so still, so sensitive, so simple it breaks me open. I walk in the woods and weep at the thought of leaving. We are all so naked and holy, so strangely connected in this unseen web, passing in and out of each other's lives.

There is a snapshot on my desk of Anne dancing in her wheelchair, living her life within limitations that many people would consider a fate worse than death. She is radiant in this picture.

Love is like gravity. It pulls you toward the center.

I called Anne. She said, "What if I'm all talk and no show?"

I pushed the words away. "You're not all talk," I told her.

She was trying to tell me something. I was moving too fast. I have us married and living together already in my mind. We are both nervous, and excited. And the country is at war.

58

Love is the great good use one person makes of another.

LORINE NIEDECKER

So after exchanging passionate love letters and phone calls with Anne for three months, I took two weeks' vacation in late January, and off I went to California. I'd prepared myself by riding the exercise bike every day and lifting weights to improve my body, getting a seventy-dollar haircut, buying new clothes, giving up caffeine and sugar, and not biting my fingers. I was in perfect shape. I imagined a magnificent two weeks of intimate closeness and romantic bliss, the beginning of a long-lasting primary relationship.

But Anne had many reservations about us that she hadn't known how to express, and of course so did I. Anne was exhausted from going to demonstrations against the Gulf War, and wasn't at the airport to meet me because she was over-whelmed with work. She sent Esther instead.

When I got to Anne's house, I noticed that the photo of me she had told me was on her desk wasn't there. She looked happy to see me, though, and we had a warm, affectionate, sexy afternoon and evening together. It was an odd situation. In some ways, we were already lovers, several months into a relationship, and in another sense we were on our first date. I was a mail-order bride.

There were no candles in the bedroom, as if the thought of a romantic night hadn't occurred to her, but we got in bed together and I tried to forge ahead without missing a beat. Anne began having leg spasms and I had the feeling she wasn't into making love with me. This was not at all the way I had imagined our first night together.

In the middle of the night—we were both awake—Anne talked about being in the hospital. She was seventeen years old. When you break your neck, they put you in a special bed that rotates you, and the pain in your neck is excruciating, and you hear the nurses saying things like, "How does this thing work?" as they prepare to flip you. Anne's mother showed up every day dead drunk.

In the morning I tried to kiss her but she turned away. She announced that it "wasn't clicking" for her. She didn't feel attracted to me. She said there was no chemistry between us.

She didn't want to be in a relationship after all, she had realized. And no, she didn't want to talk about it. Like a mirage, the whole thing had completely disappeared. I was nauseous with grief. I felt humiliated because I'd told everyone I was in love and now Anne didn't want me.

In the middle of the next night, lying beside her in bed, consumed by heartache, I suddenly *saw* that the anguish was entirely the result of thought. This thing I had wanted and imagined for months on end was suddenly not going to happen. The whole inflation had collapsed. Desire is a powerful thing. We get so set on what we think will make us happy. That's what the sorrow was about. All the energy that came from that picture of "me in love" had drained away, and all kinds of thoughts were erupting in its wake: I'm All Alone, I've Been Abandoned, Who Knows When I'll Ever Find Love Again, I'll Never Find Sex This Hot Again, I Could Have Had Ecstasy and Instead I'm Having Nothing. It was all quite comical! I began to laugh.

"There's no problem," I announced.

"Are you crazy?" Anne asked.

"No, I just suddenly realized that there's no problem."

I just lay there on my back laughing.

Seeing it so clearly, the whole construction evaporated. There was no more grief. I saw that there was no one to be humiliated except an image, and instantly that feeling was gone, too.

But then the next day I'd be swept up in the story again, and immediately the gut-wrenching nausea would return, and all the physical sensations that come with these thoughts of loss and rejection, and then the tears—everything we call grief. Amazing to *see* it all for the first time so accurately.

Within forty-eight hours I was moved out of Anne's house and staying with my friend Ginny, going through wave after wave of unpleasant sensation, feeling it in my body, listening to the thoughts that create and sustain it.

I didn't totally give up hope, either. Maybe Anne was just afraid. Maybe her feelings would change. We spent time together during the next week and sometimes we flirted and acted like lovers, and I'd think it was going to happen after all, and then she'd pull back.

I felt flashes of anger at Anne, but I saw her pain and fear, her sincerity and agony and my own responsibility too clearly. There was no one to blame. No one to defend. There was just pain—physical sensations in the body, and the thoughts that produced it. Two patterns hooking each other. In the seeing of all this, something loosened and created the space for real love to exist. There was a tenderness between the two of us. My heart kept opening. I felt astonishingly undefended.

I saw myself getting off on the idea that I was experiencing a Deep Opening in an Enlightening Way, and in the seeing I let go of that and hit rock bottom with no extras, and then instantly saw myself getting off on the idea of Hitting Rock Bottom with No Extras. Seeing the way we make something out of everything and get off on it.

One morning, very early, I picked up a woman who was hitchhiking. She was standing in the thick fog at the side of the highway in her pajamas and an overcoat. She looked terrible. Her hair was uncombed, she was disheveled and obviously ill. Her husband, she said, had been put in jail for a murder he didn't commit and she was looking for the Berkeley Women's Health Collective and then she was going home to her mother.

"Oh well," she said finally, "some women's husbands are at war. It could be worse. I should just let it go . . ."

I thought I was feeling bad until I met her.

Finally I gave up all hope of this thing with Anne working out. I decided that I didn't want a relationship with someone who either wasn't attracted to me or wasn't able to work with whatever was going on or both. I called the airline and booked an earlier flight back to New York.

I saw Anne, told her all this and she cried, talked about how afraid she was, said that she wanted to try to work with the fear and be lovers with me, although she wasn't sure if she'd be able to or what the outcome would be.

On the plane flight home I felt that *anything* was okay, life or death. The universe holds us, wondrously enough, and we are so afraid of being dropped. We fear loss, but beyond it is something else far beyond our limited imaginations so glued to our old pictures, our familiar constructions, our narrow channels.

59

*It is a very high art to live with silence and not touch it,
not manipulate it with the already known, with memory.*

JEAN KLEIN

I am back at Springwater in the snowy silence of winter. Six
more weeks, two more retreats, then back again to California
for good. That's the plan. Anne and I will be lovers. This is all
a story, I realize as I sit here telling it to myself. Something to
hold on to, to take comfort in.

There are no words finally. I touch the pot Anne made
and gave to me, following the curves with my eyes, feeling the
cool red folds of clay with my fingers and then with the end of
my arm, the exquisite defects, the secret cracks, the astonishing asymmetrical shapes, the delicious irregular line of the
lip. Crude and delicate, full of surprises.

There are long silences in our phone conversations. Nothing to say. Who are you? Who am I? I don't know anymore in
these silences. Only that we are connected, mysteriously.

❦

I descended into this Pit of Worry during the February
retreat. Here I was finally "getting somewhere" at Springwater
and like an idiot I was about to throw myself back into the
seductions of sexual lust, writing about my-*self,* and Zen (I'd

169

been having priest fantasies again). The devil was tempting me and winning. I rose to the occasion. Was ready to hurl my writing and my partially finished rakusu into the furnace, call Anne and tell her it was over. I felt sick. There were big storms of thought. I went to see Toni. It was still dark, before dawn. Words poured from my mouth in a torrent. I told her I felt torn apart. Didn't want to leave Springwater. Didn't want to sink into all these seductions that I knew in my heart were blind alleys. Except that I did want to. But I was terrified. What if . . . What if . . . What if? I told Toni I was almost (but not quite) ready to burn my writing and my rakusu, stay here and be a No Self. She laughed! (I was serious.) I went on and on, until finally I stopped talking. There was silence. Noticing that I was awaiting Toni's answer. Awaiting the solution. But she said nothing at all. There was breath. Wind. Rain dripping. Nothing else. Minutes went by. Breath. Wind. Dripping. Nothing else.

I smiled finally, because I saw. Everything lifted. There is no solution, no problem. There's just not knowing, being here, wondering, living from moment to moment. Nothing else.

Spring came during the retreat. There was a tremendous energetic shift. The snow is melting. The fields are running with water. Black crows in the rain-drenched field at dawn. A family of deer in the woods. Ever so slightly, occasional drops or flurries. And the deer, a bluish-greenish-gray. Is there a word for that color? I'm always looking for the word. And that night, white snowflakes are pouring down and blowing in all directions past my bedroom window.

Joko Beck says, "As long as our buttons are pushed, we have a great chance to learn and grow. So a relationship is a great gift, not because it makes us happy—it often doesn't—but because any intimate relationship, if we view it as practice, is the clearest mirror we can find."

At the heart of Anne, I see such light. Anne lives with her door open. The neighborhood kids visit on their way to and from school. The mailperson has lunch with her. Her space is filled with altars, sensuous arrangements of rocks and flowers, baskets of potpourri (she dries the flowers herself), the pots she makes with their curves and dents.

One morning at the marina she made me pick up all the earthworms that were lying on the asphalt, half-baked. I'd hand them to her and she'd carry them back over to the grass and the earth.

"I was worried about the earthworms all night," she told me. "They come out after the rain so they won't drown, but they're not designed for asphalt and they fry." We spent a long time rescuing them, their slippery bodies in the palms of our hands.

I watch her in my mind, dancing ahead of me in her wheelchair, turning and rolling backward, smiling at me, swooping like a bird from side to side. Turning again, she watches for the red-tailed hawk and the moon.

To be honest, to be really honest, is no easy matter, especially when one wants to believe something. The power of wanting is very strong.

60

I woke up at dawn to the sound of trees falling. I didn't know what I was hearing. There was dead silence, and then this eerie crashing. I got out of bed and looked out my window. Everything was encased in ice. It was completely silent. The power was off, I realized. There was no sound at all, and then crashing, as trees and branches fell to the ground.

It was a severe ice storm, the kind that comes once in a lifetime. The trees were falling over from the weight of the ice. I walked up to the pond. Every blade of grass in the field was encased in glass. Resplendent. It was the most ghostly and marvelous thing I ever saw.

Our driveway, which is about half a mile long, was piled with fallen trees and power lines. We had to chainsaw our way out. We had no power for a week. No heat, no running water, no flushing toilets, no lights.

We sit by candlelight around the kitchen table at night and sing old Beatles songs. We navigate the hallways with flashlights. Anne calls. I feel sad because I know in my heart it's over. We just haven't said it yet. But I can feel it. Felix and I sit in his room afterward talking. It is so dark that we can't see each other at all. Outside his window, the night sky is full of bright stars.

Even if you try to control what comes, it cannot be controlled.

DOGEN

It looks as if a hurricane has gone through. Probably half the trees are down or broken. In some areas, all the trees are down. The trails are wiped out in places.

I feel hurt by Anne, simmering in self-pitying thoughts. I feel angry. I want to hurt her back. Reject her before she rejects me. First-strike mentality.

I have decided to take a leave of absence from Springwater and go back to Oakland in the spring, come back here for the rest of the summer, and then see what happens.

There was a red fox in the field today, and then at dusk, many deer who stood and watched me pass by with great inquisitiveness and didn't run away. They are such exposed, curious beings. The air smells of pine from all the broken trees. There is the sound of dripping water. Winter is melting.

Wayu organized a women's sitting at Berkeley Zen Center and my response to it when Anne told me was startling, because it was so completely different from anything in my past. I felt no attraction to the idea, no wish to be part of it. I felt a sadness, as if something was being hurt by the exclusion of men.

I have wanted, enjoyed, and benefited from separate space in the past. But I'm looking now at how separation *is* hurtful. I'm wondering if there are other ways to find what one finds by having a women-only sitting. Maybe there aren't. I don't know.

How quickly we human beings can get polarized. I see it all the time in myself. Suddenly I'm defending some position as if my life depended on it, and afterward I'm not even sure what my position was or if I even believe it. We're all so threatened, so defended, so easily irritated by each other. And, in fact, it sounds like the Zen center is at war over this issue.

"Oh, God," I told Toni. "Here I am with my hot temper going off to a place where they're at war over feminism. I'm staying with Mike, one of the main opponents of women's sittings and a man who hasn't got a clue as to why they might actually be necessary, but I don't agree with Wayu anymore either. It's bound to be a disaster. I'll explode and do something incredibly horrible."

Toni closes her eyes. "What if you went there without all those ideas about who you are and what's going to happen? Without thinking you're 'quick-tempered' or 'bound to explode.' What if you just went there openly, not knowing?"

Oh!

My friend Ellen Chatwick in California was telling me on the phone about this women's action at the CIA building she was part of, and they all sat down in front of the building to block the entrance, all these women, and Ellen was on the end, and this man with a beard sits down next to her and holds her hand, and she doesn't know how to tell him it's a women's action. Finally she says, "Ahhh . . . I think this is a women's action," and he says, "I don't know what I am." So they get arrested together.

And Anne and I break up, by mail and phone.

61

I am sitting on my cushion in my room meditating, and I begin to imagine myself getting to Oakland and finding out that Anne refuses to talk to me. I feel more and more enraged as I think about this. I picture myself going over to her house in the middle of the night. I pound on the door. She won't answer. I'm standing on her front lawn shouting at her. I am enraged that she won't acknowledge me or let me in, that she's shutting me out. I break her bedroom window finally. One of her neighbors shoots me. I am bleeding to death on Anne's front lawn, furious. Suddenly I wake up to the fact that I'm sitting in my room at Springwater angry enough to kill. My heart is pounding, my adrenaline is flowing, and it's all a mirage.

Huge migrations going over at dawn and dusk. Dense mist floats in and erases everything, then rolls back out again just as suddenly. Rain turns to snow and back into rain. The geese honking in the dark sky, flying north into the night.

"How do they know where they're going?" somebody asked.

"Same way we know where we're going," Roger replied.

We only *think* we don't know. We imagine we have to decide.

🪷

Retreat came. I dozed off on my cushion one evening while sitting in meditation. I woke up and opened my eyes— the lighting was quite dim and I wasn't wearing my glasses— and I saw what I thought was Heather the cat walking in front of me. Good heavens, I thought, Heather has gotten into the sitting room! I was just about to reach out and grab her when I realized it was Toni's feet. Encased in her fluffy slippers, Toni was slowly making her way around the sitting room as she does during her breaks, standing briefly in front of each person as a way of being quietly together. Wouldn't she have been surprised if I had reached out and grabbed her feet!

On Day Six of the retreat, I threw my half-finished rakusu into the furnace, having finally decided that I was finished with Zen forever. I threw most of my writing into the flames with it. It was an emptying out, a cleaning house. I wanted to get rid of everything and just be quiet—do nothing, be nobody.

62

California is the end of the world. Coming back is like returning to Babylon. The Bay Area is undoubtedly one of the most cosmopolitan places on the planet, where the most advanced and highly evolved consciousness has always been found. The free-speech movement happened here, the antiwar movement, the flower children, the Gay Liberation movement, the Beatniks, the early beginnings of Buddhism and Vedanta in America. It is a place where things begin.

At the same time, the Bay Area represents the height of decadence and decline—the nauseating pinnacle of New Age capitalism, facile pop culture, a whole host of seductive inflations. The Decline of the Empire is in the air. The traffic congestion is worsening by the hour. An ever-increasing number of homeless people are everywhere, lining the streets begging, and crazy people in worn-out shoes yelling at the wind and pushing shopping carts full of rags. You see men by all the freeway underpasses in the city, holding cardboard signs that say Will Work for Food. Everyone who is not homeless lives at a frighteningly rapid pace. Some people are wearing masks now because of the pollution. There is constant noise and everything keeps growing bigger and louder.

Everything is for sale—including the so-called holistic alternatives to this nightmare. Prosperity workshops, pyramid schemes. It feels as though we're a herd of hypnotized lemmings running toward the edge.

I alternately flee and return, repulsed and attracted by the strong current of contradictions that swirls here, always ready to explode. The very ground underfoot is unreliable. In the next instant—without the slightest warning—we could all be dead, crushed, or burning up.

California has always been a kind of metaphor or unfoldment of the very malfunctioning of thought that drives human beings to seek something ever bigger and better. The pioneers came here, the gold rush, the pundits of the New Age —forward ever forward, fast forward, faster and faster, more and more. California is the last frontier—the Golden State at the edge of time, at the end of America.

By late afternoon I am in Berkeley, settling into Mike Harryman's apartment at the Zen center again. The air is warm and there is the golden light found only in California in the late afternoon. The houses in California seem to grow directly out of that light. They are pastel and seem somehow permeable and impermanent, as if they might be made from Japanese paper. They are completely different from the dark, solid houses in Rochester or Chicago. Each place on the earth is distinct and unique. The people who live in Berkeley and Oakland look and feel different from the people in Rochester. Returning to the Bay Area, I always feel a resonance. I'm home.

I am in my comfortable, loose-fitting clothes, ready for evening zazen, when I hear the purr of Anne's wheelchair down below. I look out the window and there she is coming up the walkway, looking more beautiful than I remembered. I run downstairs and we are both happy to see each other, and I want us to be lovers all over again.

It's like an alluring mirage that keeps appearing and then dissolving as soon as I get close to it. I want to feel self-righteous and victimized. I watch myself trying to exact subtle bits of retribution, trying to seduce her again.

The self, the me, can only exist in situations, and we keep creating them, don't we? I have to think of myself as something to think of myself, as Toni pointed out. There is an immense dread of nothingness, and the drama and energy of a good love affair, even a failing one, seems vastly preferable, like a habit that one returns to again and again out of fear; the fear of living without any direction.

63

My friends Naomi and Geri have adopted a baby who is HIV-positive. The baby was born addicted to crack. I feel deeply moved. So many friends of mine over the years have made the opposite choice—aborting fetuses or not adopting babies that were imperfect, wanting the perfect baby (not one like me). And here two people have willingly chosen a baby who may die before she grows up, who may have terrible problems.

"This is Avria," they tell me, introducing me to the baby. "People tell us how heroic we are," Geri says to me, "but we don't feel heroic at all. We just love this baby." Avria smiles.

Later, we are talking more about AIDS and Avria makes a sour face. Naomi turns to her. "You don't like it when we talk about AIDS, do you? Because that's not who you are, is it?"

I feel so touched. Touched that they would see perfection instead of imperfection in Avria, that they would realize that AIDS isn't who she really is, that they would choose to love this imperfect and possibly very momentary being.

One action has tremendous power to heal and transform. One choice, to care for one being, extends far beyond that one being. Their choice heals me. In loving Avria, they love the whole world.

I am enjoying sitting and living at the Zen center. Although I've thrown my rakusu away and announced (once again) the last death of my involvement in Zen, I am already secretly imagining myself sewing another and becoming a priest.

I love the benediction of Mel's bare feet on the wooden floor, the simplicity and grace of the zendo, the ambience, the smell of the incense, the aesthetics, the attention to beauty. My nervous system feels good in that room. It feels clean and warm and safe to me. I enjoy that space.

There is something comforting in the continuity and sameness of the traditional form, the fact that these chants and ceremonies go on year after year, like Mother Nature herself, endlessly repeating, yet at the same time always completely new.

I like the regularity of the practice, the fact that people gather here every morning and every evening. That steadiness seems helpful in some ways. It's a reminder that there are rhythms larger than my own, that there is a world beyond my own little drama.

Something draws me back to Zen again and again. There are attractions that cannot be explained: the comeliness of Mel's shaved head and his ears, the gratuitous elegance of the objects, the room itself, the fragrances, the sounds. Who can explain them?

You feel the care that goes into this place wherever you look. David Steindl-Rast says somewhere that "beauty is useless, superfluous, like all great things in life." (And therefore priceless.) In Toni's way there is a kind of utilitarian neorationalism that perhaps misses some of that superfluous fragrance.

But this is my old game, isn't it? Comparing, judging,

evaluating, liking and disliking, approving and disapproving. There are, I sense, inseparable strengths and weaknesses in whatever way you go, and the point ultimately is just to go.

I seem to be realizing (slowly, slowly) that I don't need to analyze and evaluate and figure out all these things. They're all just here, each with its own grace and its own weakness, and it's more important to simply experience them.

64

After a few weeks at the Zen center getting high on incense, I found myself telling Mel that I wanted to sew another rakusu. I even told him that my aspiration was to be a priest someday, because I have always known that it is. Mel said okay to the rakusu. This is the third time he's given me permission to sew one. He told me to finish sewing this one no matter how I feel, no matter what comes up. He said if/when I actually *am* a priest (functionally), then we'll both know it's time for me to become one nominally and officially as well.

So I joined another sewing class and began all over again, stitching together the tiny pieces of dark cloth. Doubts began to assail me. I began to regret my words. What am I doing? I'm not a Soto Zen priest; I'm a Springwater resident. What compels me to keep thinking I want to be a priest? Or an ordained Zen Buddhist?

Is it that I'm afraid to be alive without an anchor, a container, or an identity? Is it a refusal to be who I actually *am* and get on with it? Is it merely that the grass is always greener wherever I'm not?

When I sit alone in the backyard doing nothing, just being there under the trees, listening to traffic roar and birds singing and dogs barking and wind blowing and blood circulating and airplanes passing overhead, in that openness, I find a spaciousness and freedom that attracts me more than anything else.

This thought about what "I" should do is an old and tired loop. I stay with the bodily sensations of this moment, the sounds in the street. Nothing else is real. The thinking is merely postponing what can only happen now, with or without a rakusu, with or without becoming a priest.

65

My aunt Winifred is dying. She had a massive stroke yesterday afternoon and has been in a coma ever since. I spoke to Uncle Harold on the phone. He was crying. He said he loved me. He said with all the billions of people who die and are born each day, you have to wonder why. But something compels us to keep moving, he says.

Cocteau was once asked, If your house was burning down, what would you save? Cocteau's answer: the fire.

What is the meaning of fire?

What would happen if I stopped believing that I've got a problem? That I'm insufficient, or unenlightened, or in need of improving? What would happen if I stopped believing I'm confused? If I stopped desperately searching for the truth? What would happen if I stopped worrying about where to go next?

What would we talk about? What would we do?

I found myself in the presence of an extraordinarily quiet man, Jean Klein, a teacher of Advaita Vedanta (nondualism) and yoga. It was his presence that moved me more than anything he said, the listening stillness. Jean is a physician and musicologist from Europe who went to India years ago, had an awakening, and has been teaching ever since. He came into the room, a white-haired man probably in his seventies or eighties, sat with us for a while in silence, then took questions.

Pay close attention to your motive in coming here, he says. Is it some feeling of lack? Of wanting? Perhaps if you go into it very deeply, you can save yourself the car fare next time.

I returned the next night to be in his presence again. I am silent, finding that others ask all my questions. There is the man with the rattling mind who can't listen and can't shut up. He fills the silence with all kinds of intellectual noise. I see my own mind in him. He becomes a metaphor for that restless, anxious, self-concerned aspect of mind, for how it destroys open space. There is the woman who says she enjoys dualistic tension, opposition, bumping up against things, friction. She worries that nondualism would be boring and uniform. There is the man who wonders about the world situation. All my questions are asked if I wait in silence.

"There's too much said about meditation," Jean told us. "I think you must discover the meditation that is not meditation. You're already here. There's nowhere to go."

I feel that somatic shift happening again, my whole mind-body relaxing and opening up. I don't want to be a Zen Buddhist anymore. My body recoils at the idea of sitting through hours and days of pain and constriction. My nervous system recoils at the rigidity and artificiality of the forms. My body-mind wants to be out in the open air, wants to be free. My hand refuses to form the mudra.

I realize that I can't go on sewing this rakusu, and I can't become a Zen priest. I may, of course, do both things in time, who can predict, but right now it's seen to be unnecessary, an unwanted embellishment, a distraction. It's that subtle distinction between practicing and being, between something intentional and an effortlessness that dissolves all direction.

I told Mel I wasn't going to finish my rakusu or become a priest after all. He was disappointed. "You're not ready yet," he said.

I felt irritated.

I was walking afterward down University Avenue and I came upon a homeless addict passed out on a bench. It was an old lover of mine from years ago. I didn't wake him up.

Civilization as we know it is at an edge. Many scientists and ecologists say we have less than a decade in which to make a major change in direction before the complete destruction of complex life on this planet becomes irreversible. It is predicted that within the next ten or twenty years much of North America will be desert, that famine will be widespread here as it is in Africa today. The director general of the United Nations Environment Program, Dr. Mostafa Tolba, warns that at the current rate of destruction, "We face by the turn of this century an environmental catastrophe as complete and as irreversible as any nuclear holocaust." We are at the end or the beginning of the world.

Deep-ecologist John Seed says that nothing but a miracle would be of any use at this time. Not very likely? Maybe not, he tells us, but consider the miracle of being descended from a fish that left the water to walk on the land.

It seems as if we need a transmutation in consciousness on the level of that quantum evolutionary leap from water to land. Obviously, this is not something we can engineer or make happen. It comes, if it does at all, by grace. We cannot know whether or when it will happen, or even what it is that we are weaving. Technological expansion, urbanization of the planet, even nuclear or environmental holocaust, may be as "natural" as thunder and lightning. Death, after all, is part of life, as are chaos, impermanence, and ceaseless change. We only think we know anything.

I don't believe anymore that there are any easy answers. It all seems much messier and more complex to me now than it once did, when I neatly divided the world into good guys and bad guys and thought I was on the right side. Now I don't know. I don't think there is a right side, and I've discovered that the bad guys are me as surely as the good guys, and it's hard to separate the light from the dark.

Sometimes I wonder if it makes any sense at all to think of "solving" our global problems. The earth, like any living organism, will eventually die. The sun will explode. There's no way to "win" the battle or to know what's beyond our limited human vision. Maybe we should just forget about recycling and social justice and meditative inquiry and all the rest. But then I think of Avria, that tiny baby born with HIV and addicted to crack, and I think of Geri and Naomi adopting Avria and caring for her with such love and enthusiasm even though she may die or turn out to be brain-damaged or who knows what. It doesn't make sense to think we can "solve" anything if by solving we mean making it go as we imagine or think it should go. But love makes sense. And it seems that when you see clearly, love is what happens. If you really see a fly, you don't swat it. If you really see a flower, you don't step on it. If you really see Avria, you don't abandon her. If you really see the world, you take care of it. Even though it might blow up, and even though eventually it *will* blow up.

66

On Saturday I went to my old karate school, where I studied for many years, to see one of my old friends there test for her second-degree black belt. This woman was a total wimp when she started. I mean, she was thin and frail and she'd crumple completely under pressure. She'd cower when attacked, and she even ran off the dojo floor in tears once during an early belt test. You would *never*, ever have imagined that this woman could become a black belt. But there she was, transformed. She had this gentle, relaxed presence (not egotistical at all, but an absence of self-consciousness or self-deprecation). She was so natural, so strong. It gave me hope. If Bonnie Price can be a second-degree black belt, then maybe the Heart of the World can be salvaged.

My friend Ginny had a ritual for her fiftieth birthday. There were about thirty women there. We sat in a circle and told about how we knew her, and what she meant to us. It was like unfolding a tapestry, as one woman after another spoke. Then we lifted her up on our fingertips and rocked her in the air and sang to her. It was a ritual in which we ushered her into her crone years. I was struck by how much has changed in my lifetime around women, lesbianism, aging, menopause. Most of these were forbidden topics when I was growing up, discussed—if at all—only in hushed whispers. Now they are discussed freely; celebrated, even; enjoyed. I was struck by the difference between this ritual and those at the Zen center. This ritual was spontaneous, unscripted, improvisational theater. Like the Indian sand paintings, it was a one-time happening. It was alive, and seemed to function as a vehicle for seeing and listening, rather than a rote occurrence that one performs from memory, obligation, and habit.

I dreamed I was in a huge cathedral doing the stations of the cross as a kind of altar girl or attendant to the priest, who is performing some liturgical rite at each altar we come to, and I'm carrying a roll of toilet paper in the procession (I almost wrote: a role of toilet paper). This must be a mistake, I think. I should be carrying something else. Reb gets up at the main pulpit and begins delivering this strong antisex speech. Women get up one by one, jeering him, and leave. But I stay. What he's saying makes sense to me. There is something about Toni in the dream, too: realizing that Toni is just like us, that she has exactly the same mind, the only difference is that she doesn't identify with it.

In the shower, I recalled the famous Zen koan:

Ummon was asked, "What is Buddha?"
Ummon replied, "Toilet paper."

A friend of mine once said to me—during a discussion about the divinity of Jesus—that he could never accept someone who had a poop chute as God. I told him that in Zen, God *is* a poop chute.

My friend Elaine is doing hospice work now on the AIDS ward of a hospital with poor people. She massages the legs that are as thin as her arms and covered with sores—not open, and thus safe to touch, but still she washes her hands over and over when she gets home. She sits with a dying black drug addict as he eats his dinner and vomits simultaneously into a wastebasket.

It is interesting to note that I haven't "exploded" or done anything horrible over the various conflicts going on here at the Zen center over women's sittings. I have in fact been playing almost a kind of mediator role, able to hear and sincerely understand both sides.

The blossoms from the fruit trees blow in my open window and settle on the floor of my room. Bees fly in, too. I listen to Bach cello suites in bed and idle away time.

One afternoon I am meditating, or *thinking* I am, and there is a sense of being intensely present, and then the thought comes up: "I'm on the verge of total clarity"—sort of like being on the brink of an orgasm—and then, "What if the phone rings?" Anxiety shoots through me and I am bracing against the imagined interruption, and the anticipated loss of clarity that will result. Suddenly there is waking up and seeing that the ringing phone can only be a problem when thought imagines "me" getting to some big spiritual breakthrough in the future, in time (which is imagination), if I can just be undisturbed long enough to get there. The whole thing is a story! It's a thought that "I'm on the verge of total clarity," it's a thought that "I'm not enlightened," it's a thought that "I could be" and that "This will take time," it's a thought that there's a "me" separate from the rest of life to whom this is happening, it's a thought that the phone might ring. Sometimes I just burst out laughing. It *all* unravels!

> *Those who have great realization of delusion are buddhas; those who are greatly deluded about realization are sentient beings.*
>
> DOGEN

Can awareness be sustained? Does it have to keep disappearing, sometimes for long periods? Where does this question come from? Is it thought again, conjuring up time, wanting something, something permanent, something for me?

67

My article about disability and Buddhist practice came out in a Buddhist magazine. Many Buddhists with disabilities wrote to say, "Thanks for telling it like it is."

Mel called me into his office. He was upset because I had talked about the Zen center and the resistance here to ramping the zendo. He felt I had exaggerated things and distorted his motives.

"Do you imagine that people here are actually prejudiced against disabled people?" he asked me.

189

"Yes," I replied. "There's definitely discrimination and prejudice."

"No," he assured me, "there isn't. People want to do everything they can to help people in such situations."

I was blown away.

"I feel dumped on," he said. "You look for the holes in people and go after them. You use words very carelessly."

I could see that he was genuinely hurt. Suddenly I realized that he was a person, like me, and that what I had said about him actually affected him.

"You say in your article that Zen overemphasizes posture," Mel continued. "You can't possibly emphasize posture too much."

"Awareness isn't dependent on posture," I asserted. "Look at Anne. She slumps. She doesn't have the muscles to sit erect. Does that mean she can't realize the truth?"

"Of course not," Mel replied. "Perfect posture for her is slumping. You always have to adjust it to your own circumstances."

"But how do you think she feels when almost every talk you give focuses on posture, and always sets up this position that she can never get into as the ideal way?"

"Where do you get your authority to speak like this?" he asked.

"My authority?" I couldn't believe what I was hearing.

"Yes. You're marching with your banner in such a self-righteous way. Even though you have a lot of experience, you still have much to taste and accept. And yet you're ready to ignore the whole Buddhist tradition, the wisdom of centuries. The difficulties are part of the practice, part of what you go through in order to mature. Your practice isn't mature enough to speak about these things. There is a lot you haven't realized yet. Your idealism is still leading the way."

I felt discounted and put down. It seemed that my experiences were not being taken seriously, my viewpoint was not being valued or listened to. The image of me as a person who is advancing nicely on the path was being crushed. Waves of emotion passed through me. I could see a story taking shape in my mind, a story about what a jerk Mel is, how I'm right and he's blind as a bat.

Who was hurt?

I felt angry and defensive because it's not true what he says, it's outrageous arrogance, and I felt afraid because it is true. I wanted revenge, wanted to insult him back. But maybe I already had insulted him.

I felt terrible.

Mel didn't look very happy either.

He has taken me back three times, and three times I have rejected him. The thought went through my mind that I would never come to him as a teacher ever again. But I can see that this is only a picture in the mind and in another moment the kaleidoscope will shift, the pieces will tumble and reform, and I might be sewing another rakusu.

We talked some more, and finally I got up to leave. We hugged. There was pain but also tenderness between us. I felt touched, hurt, angry, sad, ashamed, and self-righteous, all in one messy moment. Mel's right. I've been arrogant and thoughtless. I haven't seen him or life accurately. I've acted out of ideas and opinions. I've hurt people. And if it *bothers* me to be told that my practice isn't mature yet, then obviously it's true.

68

I met a man named Albert who is staying for a few days at Anne North's house. Albert is close to sixty years old and was once employed by Kodak at a highly paid job, but some thirty years ago he walked out. He is a Christian who decided to take Jesus seriously, to test out in real life the way of living that Jesus advocates. Own nothing. Sell what you possess, give to the poor, take nothing with you, do unto the least of these, have faith, be like the lilies of the field. The gospel as it really is, which is a radical message. Albert quit his job and gave away all his money and all his material possessions.

He engages in nonviolent resistance against nuclear war and other injustices, then he spends time in prison, sometimes a year at a time, usually in noisy, crowded circumstances with no privacy or quiet at all. When he's not in prison, he lives mostly at a Benedictine monastery where they seem to regard him as one of the family, although he is not a Catholic. He owns nothing.

His presence is quiet and gentle. What strikes me about him is that his life is so completely not about himself. He doesn't seem focused on the kinds of things that I seem caught up in most of the time, like what "I" should do to be happy, or get enlightened. I guess that's true of Toni, too, and Joko, and Mel. They aren't wrapped up in self-concern. I feel very tired of living on that level of endless self-concern that goes nowhere and seems so sick in the face of what's happening on this planet, both the awesome wonder that's transpiring every minute and the awesome horror that's unfolding and moving us rapidly toward annihilation.

When Albert quit his job at Kodak and "divested" himself of everything, he decided to experiment and find out if the scriptures were true in saying that his needs would be provided for. You test an idea out by giving your life to it, he said. There's no other way.

Albert spoke of how painful it was to him to see how money was spent here in the Bay Area, to see the wealth and the lifestyle and the hypocrisy; the way genuinely radical insights become so quickly and easily co-opted. He had seen a bumper sticker that said something like, Subvert the Dominant Paradigm—"on the back of a new Volvo," he scoffed.

"It's not that poverty is desirable," he said to me, "it isn't. It's horrible. But if your heart is truly open, poverty is more or less unavoidable."

I feel like a tourist, like those I see in the national parks who turn me off, only my tourism is internal. I go sightseeing in the realms of meditation practices and spiritual trips, in search of ever-better experiences and states of being for the me to possess, snapping pictures and swapping stories as I go, missing the profundity of what's in front of me. The mind keeps conjuring up where I'll be next. But I'll always be right here, wherever I am. There's nowhere else to go except in thought.

69

"Oh, fuck. I hate being a quadriplegic," Anne said when I was over at her house this morning. She had just dropped the telephone. "I'm trying to do it really good in this life so I won't ever have to do it again." She sails down the hall, the phone dragging along behind her, the cord tangled in one of her wheels, flashing me a huge grin.

We went to a Japanese tea shop and had some kind of smoky green tea. Afterward we took a long walk at the marina and watched the pelicans. As we were leaving, Anne pulled the van over to the side of the road. "Look," she said. In the marshes, there was a great white egret standing on its long, delicate legs, fishing. We sat there a long while in silence watching it.

Back at her house afterward, I proposed to her again.

"You're not serious and I know it," she said.

"Maybe I am," I replied.

"We'd have to get it annulled in twenty-four hours, Joan."

I still imagine our lovemaking holding some immense healing power for me. I can't bear the thought that we never got to do it, not even once. I can't stand being shut out, not wanted.

I told her I was beginning to conceive of a book based on my journals.

"Oh, God," she said.

"I'll use pseudonyms," I told her. "Jane Doe, quadriplegic dancer. No one will recognize you."

"Can I wear sunglasses too?"

We ended up in her kitchen kissing passionately. Or perhaps it was more like kissing dispassionately. There was no love in it, no adoration. It was some desire for closeness, or I don't know what.

"This changes everything," I said.

"I guess I want to think that it doesn't change a thing," Anne replied.

But I didn't hear her.

Kenny was watching butterflies in the garden through his binoculars when I arrived. It was almost the end of my time in California. Kenny is an urban gardener who tends a variety of large plots all over Berkeley. He is a gay physician and acupuncturist whose practice is primarily with AIDS patients. His own lover died of AIDS a few years ago.

I told him, "It was my worst fear when I got into meditation that I would become a kind of spectator, and now I find that whatever happens appears to be just a play of phenomena, essentially purposeless. We assume injustice is bad, but it becomes very hard in the end to discern what is good and what is evil. The words hold no meaning anymore. Simpleminded political thinking that used to captivate me seems so apparently false and unreal to me now. You cure one problem and the cure creates a whole new disease."

"Um." Kenny nods and smiles appreciatively. Kenny loves uncomfortable paradoxes.

"If someone had said this to me a few years back, I would have been outraged," I said. "Now it seems true."

Kenny tells me that he's been realizing that AIDS may be one of the greatest blessings of our time, because it's an epidemic that attacks reproductive-age people at a time of overpopulation when we obviously need a huge population decimation in order to survive. Every day there are a quarter of a million more people than there were the day before. Within sixty years the earth's population will have almost doubled from what it is today. Kenny looks intensely thoughtful. "But people don't want to think that," he says finally. "We all want to live forever." He grins his dark, ironic grin that delights in all possibilities.

It so often seems to be the case that when we see the falsity of one conditioned idea (for example, that women are inferior to men), we then replace it with a different idea (for example, that women are equal to men, or that the feminine is superior). Then we get invested in that, and can't question it. I'm becoming increasingly aware of how those of us with "progressive" politics are often as rigid in our thinking as the right-wing, Bible-banging opposition is. I like our ideas better, so it's harder to see them as also being nothing more than concepts imposed on reality, another set of nonnegotiable assumptions, but they so often are. Real healing is freedom from all habit patterns and fixed beliefs, not creating new and better ones to get stuck in.

Kenny sings to me an old Shaker song. His voice is simple and clean, like Shaker furniture. We sit together in silence afterward. The phone rings. One of his patients is dying. He has to leave for the hospital. He packs me a brown bag full of homegrown vegetables, stuffs his stethoscope in his pocket, and off he goes.

At evening zazen that night I ran into a friend from long ago who told me that Sophie Cardarelli, my therapist back when I sobered up, has an inoperable brain tumor and is dying. She gives me Sophie's telephone number in San Anselmo and I call Sophie up that night. I haven't spoken to her in more than a decade.

"Is this Joan with the arm?" Sophie asks. Her speech is slow and slightly slurred, as if she has cerebral palsy.

I arrange to go and visit her the following day. She greets me at the door. She is thirty pounds heavier from the steroids, and she walks slowly and with difficulty, but she is happy to see me and still cracking jokes.

Her mother and sister have come from New Jersey to take care of her, and her mother talks about her as if she weren't in the room. "Sophie is incontinent now," her mother whispers loudly to me. "She should have been dead a year ago, but she's still here."

Sophie tries, unsuccessfully, to identify the family photos on the refrigerator as her mother corrects her. Sophie swallows about ten pills and we adjourn to the backyard where we can be alone together. She holds my arm, stroking it and looking at it.

"You don't have to hide it anymore," she tells me.

Her brain seems to be locked into old grooves, like my arm, which was the centerpiece of our therapy work, and it's as if the tape is still playing. My arm seems also to be almost metaphorical—a kind of symbolic embodiment of imperfection and loss, and thus of Sophie's own situation. I feel strangely detached from this funny arm of mine as it rests in Sophie's hands, under her gaze. It isn't me, and yet—sure enough—it's still there, still attracting attention and meaning, some strange koan that won't let me go.

Sophie seems slightly mentally retarded, and yet she can describe her own situation with perfect lucidity. At one point in the conversation, in fact, she wonders whether it makes sense to keep fighting for life under these circumstances, and she describes herself as "a once-brilliant woman who is now retarded."

Our roles have reversed in a strange way. Whatever it is that I love about her, it is beyond the intellect or the memory or the body—all of those things that can perish and be destroyed—it is something that no tumor can touch. Saying good-bye, I know I will never see her again.

"I love you," I say.

She holds my arm between her hands. "I love you," she tells me.

70

I've decided to drive my geriatric Toyota back to Springwater. I call Anne every day on the road. I am already imagining myself coming home to her in the fall.

I stopped in Chicago to see my mother and one afternoon I went alone to visit Uncle Harold. He walks with a cane and loses his balance. I had mailed him a copy of Toni's book, and he had read it.

"You didn't think I would, did you?" he asks. "Well, I did. She sounds too much like Mary Baker Eddy for my taste."

He was raised by Christian Scientists.

He took me to lunch at a vegetarian restaurant near the retirement home, and we sat afterward in the garden at the home near the tree he had planted for Winifred after she died.

"Her ashes are under it," he told me quietly. "Nobody knows that. But they are."

We sat there beside that tree and talked about politics, religion, homosexuality, Henry Kissinger, U.S. foreign policy, abortion, and women's rights. I could not believe we were doing it. We were discussing every loaded issue imaginable, and yet—to my utter amazement—we didn't quarrel or get angry. In fact, we hardly even seemed to disagree. I am hearing or listening on a different level, without defenses and assumptions, and so is he. If Uncle Harold and I can talk like this, there's hope for the world.

71

So here I am back at Springwater. Watching the moon rise in the pond. Couldn't you be doing this a little bit better? the mind asks. Couldn't the colors be a little bit brighter? Is this really clarity? Are you sure you're doing it right?

"What is this about clarity?" I ask Toni. "Who wants it? I feel utterly depressed. Who cares if I can hear the birds cheeping? What is all this clarity stuff, anyway?"

"So have you stopped looking for it yet?" Toni asks.

It's such a tiny shift in the mind between wanting and enlightenment. Letting go of the dream, having *nothing* to look forward to anymore. What relief! What immensity! And yet how we dread it!

"Can the wanting be there like the heartbeat?" Toni asks. "Just hear it, feel it." Wanting, wanting, wanting. The pulsation of human psychology. Without getting sucked into the content of it, the particular object(s) we imagine will make us happy.

> *Wanting to wake up*
> *Wanting to be loved*
> *Wanting to know what to do*
> *Wanting the judging to stop forever*
> *Wanting enlightenment to be a state of feeling good all*
>   *the time*

Wanting world peace and the end of all suffering
Wanting a quiet mind
Wanting Anne North
Wanting Clarity
Wanting to stop wanting

Wanting
Wanting
Wanting

I remember again that last visit with Erik Hummingbird before he died of AIDS. He was in the hospital, wearing an oxygen mask. There were a bunch of us there who had known one another over many years. Erik, who always threw amazing parties, was still playing host from his hospital bed, orchestrating the pouring out of cranberry-juice cocktails into paper cups with ice, one for each of us. That cranberry-juice cocktail was an awakening moment for me. I realized that this was all there was. There was no future here, nothing to become, nothing to unearth or attain, nowhere further to go. The dream was over. There was nothing at all to look forward to. There was just this juice in this paper cup, and these people. All of us were acting just as we always had acted, except for the one tiny difference that all of us were aware of the preciousness of one another and of that cranberry juice. That juice was Holy Communion.

I never saw Hummingbird again.

Jean Klein says to pay careful attention to the moment of waking up in the morning. So I have been. It's very revealing to see how the self and the world get reconstructed every morning by the mind. The memory wakes up and the thought of my life reappears. I am Joan Tollifson. Oh, yes. Her! I have to step back into my part. "Joan," who is working so hard to become enlightened. Suddenly there is a huge task before me, to manage all of this, which is obviously unmanageable, to control what is obviously uncontrollable, to get somewhere and become somebody and do something. It feels like this huge boulder I have to pick up again and carry.

The world here is alive with desire. The wild grasses humming and crackling with crickets and grasshoppers, thousands of tiny butterflies fluttering over the flowers, dragonflies basking on the warm rocks. Frogs float in the water, their long legs drifting behind them, their yellow throats swelling with sound. Their dissonant croaks and trills fill the air. At night, fireflies flash out of the darkness. Electrical storms pass through. Stentorian thunder crashes. Lightning flares illuminating the landscape and plunging it back into darkness.

I called Anne and got her answering machine, and she didn't call me back for days. Finally she did call. It turns out that she has a new lover. I hear this and there is more grieving and anger to move through, more disappointment.

I wake up depressed. I see that I want to wallow in my story: "Poor-Me, I've Been Screwed Again." There's a reluctance to let it go, because that would mean I was all upset over nothing at all. I want to keep the story going because it's *my* story, and if *it's* nothing but thin air, then that means *I'm* nothing but thin air. This clutching panic arises, and the thought that it *can't* all just be nothing. I've invested enormous time and energy in this drama of my suffering: analyzing it, writing about it, thinking about it, talking about it, feeling it. To see that it has no reality at all seems like a huge loss. We don't want to let go of our suffering, our self-image as victim, the importance it gives to us. What would I do (or be) without it?

Retreat came. I coordinated and also did Toni's daily massage. Getting down to the bones beneath the image, the soft, aging body, the blue veins on the legs, the pink skin on the scalp. The body is so vulnerable, so fleeting.

I'm recognizing how impermanent and perishable we are, how fragile our whole sexual dream is. In the end, it crumbles, literally, to dust. I don't think I've ever looked this reality quite so squarely in the face before, without moving away from it, or feeding myself reassurances.

I don't want reassurances at this point. I want to see the truth. Somehow for me these days there's a much more profound power in allowing things to not be okay. All my life I've tried to be cheerful and funny, tried not to be sad, tried not to be a cripple, and suddenly I find something liberating in seeing that right now I'm not happy, and maybe I'm not attractive either.

Of course I know that beauty is in the eye of the beholder

and that I have been seen as desirable, and probably will be again. But I want the space to be depressed, to *see* the ugliness, the pain, the ways in which I'm not perceived as an attractive woman (by Anne, by society at large, by myself), and the sorrow in that. For once in my life I want to allow myself to be an ugly, depressed cripple. Is it so terrible, really, to be an ugly, depressed cripple?

It's fascinating to watch people around you squirm when you try to do that. No, no . . . you're not ugly . . . you're not a cripple . . . cheer up . . . stop!

These specters that we think will be the death of us turn out to be straw tigers in the end. What we are fundamentally does not get hurt, rejected, or killed.

Retreat was hard. Lots of depression that never let up until the last hour of the last day when I must have finally stopped wanting it to let up or imagining that it might. Then something shifted. Again the expansiveness of not wanting anything. Of exactly this, as it is.

After the retreat, Toni was naked on the massage table— I was giving her the final massage—and Kyle had arrived and was sitting on the couch, and the three of us were talking, having a very animated conversation. It was strangely intimate and unusual, and made me feel happy.

72

Will I stay here in the fall or return to California? I wonder. The wind blows. The leaves shimmer in the light. Watching thought trying to figure it all out.

Toni asked me if I could just be with the energy of being

nobody without doing anything with it: not needing to fight someone, help someone, fall in love with someone, write books, or anything at all. Was it possible to just let it be?

There are moments of presence, of listening without any ideas or plotlines, without self-center. And then I am sucked back into the swirling vortex of thought, looking for the answer again, wallowing in my confusion. Sometimes all of this no longer disturbs me; it is merely the tide coming in and going out and nothing at all is wanted anymore, no improvement. Everything becomes transparent.

I sit by the pond at nightfall until long after dark, a dance of bats mirrored in the water. The new moon hangs in the sky, a thin crescent of light. Cattails loom by the rim of the pond with their huge dark heads. There is immensity in this night. Space around and within all objects. No solidity, no division. I look for myself and no one is here. We are all one process, happening. Thought creates appearance and density, but in this vast night it is seen through completely. There is *nothing!*

The next day I search for my experience, my enlightenment. Is this it? Maybe not quite. Do I still have it? Where is it? How can I get it back? Am I enlightened or not?

If you try to attain enlightenment as if you see a bright star in the sky, it will be beautiful and you may think, "Ah, this is enlightenment," but that is not enlightenment. That understanding is literally heresy. Even though you do not know it, in that understanding you have the idea of material only. Dozens of your enlightenment experiences are like that—some material only, some object of your mind, as if through good

practice you found that bright star. That is the idea
of self and object. It is not the way to seek for enlighten-
ment.

SUZUKI ROSHI

People pass through. Didn't Thoreau say something
about how, if you just stay in one spot, the whole world will
pass by in front of you? It feels that way here. People arrive
and depart. Lovely people. They come into your life and then
they vanish—for a month, or for a year, or forever. You imagine that you'll never survive the departure of some particular
person you've grown to love, and then he or she goes and
someone else you love shows up. When I can just relax and go
with it, it's a wonderful lesson. What we need is always present. Is presence itself.

Here, the song of the wood thrush at dusk can break your
heart, it is so pure. The secretive thrush always remains unseen.
There is only the liquid, flutelike song, ascending and descend-
ing, each note perfect and exquisite. I run out to it at twilight
as to a lover.

In the woods, the owl flies out of the trees and lands on a
branch above me. I look up into her feathered face and her
great dark eyes, and she gazes down on me. We remain like
that, watching each other for a long while, until finally she
lets out a primordial cry and flies off between the trees.

73

There has been a shift inside me. I notice that I don't feel
wounded or insulted when I hear the word *cripple*, when I
encounter some backward attitude to homosexuality, or some

sexist behavior. I see it for what it is, but without the sense of personal injury. There is more compassion for other people, more sensitivity to them. I can choose my battles more carefully, and fight them with less heat, and thus with less of the exaggeration, defensiveness, and hostility that tends to make others ever more locked into their positions instead of giving them space to hear and discover for themselves what's happening, to reexamine and change.

I'm more conscious of the goodness in people. All the ways that I *have* been treated with care and respect—the fact that most people seem to trust my capabilities despite my disability, the ways many men sincerely want to support women in getting stronger and being more empowered, the ways straight people in my life—like my parents—have accepted my lesbianism or my bisexuality, and how my mother has fought for gay rights. I mean, it isn't as if my entire existence has been oppressive. The vast majority of my experiences with other human beings are enormously positive.

Yes, people are oppressed in real and terrible ways. If political work is about becoming aware of the mechanics and particularities of such oppression, and working to change things, then maybe that's constructive. If it degenerates into getting off on the victim role, on being the most oppressed person, then it becomes false. You find yourself wanting to tell the story of how hard it is to be a woman, disabled, or gay— wanting some kind of unconditional sympathy and respect. You begin to see injustices when they aren't actually there. You are always fighting, angry, sure you're right.

What is absent with insight is the personal identification with, and dependency upon, a particular outcome, which inevitably distorts our ability to see and act intelligently. This isn't some kind of mystical nonsense, but an ability to be with reality when it disappoints us, either in minor ways, like waking up and finding no milk for your coffee, or in larger ways, like suffering from discrimination or prejudice of some kind, or in extreme ways, like being starved or tortured or put to death. If we don't get the outcome we want in any given situation, if life doesn't go as we think it should, then what happens to us inwardly? Are we—ultimately—dependent on this body? On reality matching our ideals? To the extent that we are, human life will be confusing and disappointing. To see reality as it actually is, without moving away, is an enormous act of healing and transformation.

Not wanting or not being identified is not a state of passively accepting injustices, dissolving into some kind of formless bliss and not caring about the environment or social justice or whatever. Because if you see clearly, you don't stand by and let yourself or anyone else be run down by a truck (literally or figuratively).

It is a struggle to be personally honest, to expose yourself and take risks. And I have begun to realize that it is another kind of struggle, and risk, to go beyond the need to tell my particular story and have it validated and confirmed, to get beyond all of this thought that feels so real, the whole huge drama of me and my terrible suffering. A Tibetan rinpoche, who had seen a great deal of hardship himself, once commented that "all lives are the same."

Do we bristle at that statement?

"You think you're so different," someone told me recently, "but you're not really different."

Everything in me rebelled. Yes, I am. I'm different. I'm special. I don't fit in. I'm better (or worse). I'm me. We identify with what we think and say, with our history, our body, our various labels, our pain. We see any behavior that hurts us as a willful, intentional attack on us personally (or on those we identify with), rather than as an impersonal manifestation of conditioning, often a pervasive social pattern of conditioning and imagery that the whole society is caught up in, that isn't anyone's personal choice. Does the murderer *choose* his behavior any more than the murder victim?

74

Uncle Harold had a massive heart attack. They brought him back from the dead. He survived. "During my noisy ride to the hospital," he writes, "the paramedic said, 'There he goes, his eyes are rolling back.' For me, things were getting black and I couldn't have been more peaceful. Maybe I missed my chance—no pearly gates or anything. Everybody was wonderful. Found out later that your mother and the clinic nurse, Linda Jo, sat up till three in the morning. The nurses were wonderful especially. Washed you *all over* and cuddled you. Whew. The ceiling was a typical soundproofing pattern; the walls pink with a television and clock. Somehow, the clock and television got to be on the floor and the ceiling became the wall. They would go back to normal and I would stare and stare at them to catch them in transition. No luck. When the ceiling was the wall, two of the loveliest little ladies would appear, dressed in spring clothes of the 1920s so sweet and charming. They would stay around and just disappear into the wall-ceiling. The doctor would hand me a yellow-ruled paper and ask me to write something. Harold Osborne, I would write proudly, but it came out an up-and-down squiggle, but I was still proud. Love and kisses, Harold."

The letter is typed, except for his name—Harold—which is written in shaky script. And there is a photograph of him enclosed with the letter. I place it on my desk.

I found old photographs of Uncle Harold when I packed up my things before coming here, photographs of a handsome young man in a ten-gallon cowboy hat standing beside his bride, Winifred, whom he courted for seven years—a winsome young actress who had a graduate degree in mathematics and was a talented athlete. They had gone west on their honeymoon. It was before I was born. Now Winifred is dead, and Harold is an old man with a hearing aid and a pacemaker.

In the same box, I found a photograph of my mother sitting up in bed. She looks very young, and she's nursing this tiny, tiny baby.

75

We had a staff meeting and Felix, who is always so soft-spoken and quiet, blew up at Paul, screaming at him. It was received so spaciously, like the times when I've blown up here. People drop it so quickly and completely, and I realize how rare that is, how precious. I know that everyone here is looking at how we react, and not just going off and building up our case against the others. That's what I love.

At the same time, I worry that Springwater isn't enough. It's too uncertain, laissez-faire, nothing. I worry that it will turn out to be the wrong choice and I'll wake up thirty years from now and realize I ruined my whole life. I am afraid of being stuck *here* (anywhere), afraid of becoming ordinary or commonplace, afraid of being depended upon, of having more and more responsibility.

I spend large parts of every day imagining where else I could be where I'd be happier. I've done this for years, and I see it happening, but it's so compelling and addictive that it just keeps right on happening. I don't want to stop.

The thought of staying in New York and eventually giving up my California driver's license is almost too painful to bear. It's amazing the attachment I feel to that license, amazing to see how I am identified with "California," whatever that is. I only have to think of that driver's license and I am filled with emotion.

Stay or go. Stay or go. I reach moments of utter clarity where it seems perfectly apparent what I'm going to do, then within twenty-four hours it flips completely to the opposite.

Mind bubbles.

And such a hunger to settle, to *be* somewhere—some place or some way—and not leave. The morning I left California for Springwater the very first time, I went for dokusan with Mel. It was before dawn, and I bowed to him and sat facing him in the tiny candlelit room where we had met so many times before. He gave me a figure from the altar to take with me on my journey.

"What is settling?" I asked him.

"Settling is waking up moment to moment," he replied.

76

I asked Paul if he feels he's still growing here, since he often seems unhappy and talks frequently of leaving, and he says that he doesn't think in terms of growth. All that personal fulfillment and development stuff isn't relevant, he says, all that matters is kindness. Are we becoming any kinder? The wind was blowing in the trees when he said it, it was dusk, and I felt so touched.

I, unfortunately, am still pursuing growth.

People pass through and talk of the programs they're embarked on to become therapists, Rolfers, naturopaths, nurses, whatever. And I seem to be embarked on a program to become nobody. At the end of it you have nothing. You are nowhere. You have no future. There is no you. It doesn't pay at all.

"It's a very difficult program," Felix jokes. "Most people who enroll in it drop out."

Sharon made me a really decadent chocolate cake for my birthday and everyone sang off-key to me and I felt well-loved and ate too much and turned forty-three. Today it rained a little and tonight I listened to music in Paul's room, then walked in the fields at twilight. Everything smelled so sweet from the rain. The frogs were singing and the mosquitoes were biting.

Anne sent me a basket full of flowers that she had dried for my birthday and the scent permeates my room along with the rain smells from the window. I was thinking today that Anne was the perfect person with whom to do what we *actually* did together—everything that was illuminated and healed in terms of disability, that I no longer fear the word *cripple,* or the fact of being a cripple; everything that was revealed about fantasy and rejection and hurt. She wasn't at all an appropriate person for what we *imagined* doing together. And oddly enough, what I realized today is that we couldn't have done what was real without the fabrication, without the part that was bogus. So I can say in retrospect that it was all a mistake or a huge delusion, but actually it was what it was. Our ideas are just concepts. The hand reaches for the pillow in the middle of the night regardless of what we think. It cannot be talked about on the level of right and wrong. The separations and evaluations exist only in thought.

But this all sounds too pretty and neat, and actually I'm a mess. I go to bed depressed. I wake up depressed. I feel sad because I don't know where home is, because I fell in love with someone who is unable to love me, and because I know I would have rejected her if she had wanted me.

People have such funny ideas about what a meditation-retreat center is, or what it must be like to live in one. They think it must be a peaceful, idyllic life. Low stress, lots of bliss. But actually, in so many ways, it's often quite the opposite. Being in solitude and silence much of the time, being stripped of all your habitual escapes and your comforting ideas and left face-to-face with bare-bones actuality can be anything but blissful and idyllic.

Being in community, living/working with the same people constantly, not always the people you'd choose, dealing with an endless stream of guests, living in a place that isn't exactly your home because it's a retreat center, and the intensity of doing this kind of inner work in such an exposed and persistent way is not always easy. People come in touch here with profound depression, loneliness, despair, and sorrow.

It's as if I'm contacting something that's always been

there, and no longer being able to move away from it. It's the sadness of being alive. It has nothing to do really with Anne or any other external circumstances. It's the primal pain of being embodied: separate, misunderstood, incomplete by definition. It's that deep, central grief that so many spiritual masters speak of, the wound that opens to grace.

But sometimes it doesn't open and we just lie there in bed feeling horrible. All the pictures of how we're supposed to be don't help. When I was young, I imagined myself growing up and turning into Albert Schweitzer. I'd be a doctor in Africa or a social worker in the slums. I'd save people in need. I never imagined myself at forty-three cleaning toilets and spending my off-hours gnawing on my fingers until they bled, unable to stop. If I imagined myself back then as a contemplative, it was serene and silent, not tortured and neurotic. I wasn't engaging in self-mutilation and obsessive worry about where to go. I was enlightened, peaceful, helpful. It's funny, I know, but sometimes I can't seem to laugh. I just want to cry.

77

A big storm is blowing in. The sky is getting darker, the wind wilder. Thunder is rumbling in the distance, coming closer. The rain starts. It grows very dark. Thunder explodes and lightning bolts flash across the sky. Rain pours down in sheets. The trees are whipped by the wind. The rain turns to hail. Felix walks out into it, and from a window above, I watch the white hailstones landing in his black hair.

My mother came to visit. We sat in silence a lot, on the wooden benches overlooking the fields, just being together quietly, wordlessly, watching the clouds pass.

After she left, Felix took me canoeing on Hemlock Lake at sunset. The boat slides soundlessly through the water. I watch the shapes of light moving for sheer pleasure, without any idea of attainment or purpose. It's all so effortless here, rocking delicately under the new moon and the red clouds. Herons are fishing in the distance, by the opposite shore. We move closer and coast along near the shoreline, through the reflections of fallen trees, damaged by the ice storm, their dark shapes rippling. Fish leap out of the water in silver flashes of light, and swim through the reflections. The melodious song of wood thrushes floats out over the lake. We drift in silence on the dark water. Felix spots a bald eagle sitting high up in a broken tree. We glide closer and look through the binoculars. The eagle appears wounded. We move away finally. I look at Felix. Our eyes meet, universes of light. Afterward, when we got home and it was dark, Felix massaged me. His warm hands on my sleepy body.

My friend Ginny in Berkeley called the next morning and urged me to come back home to California and move into her house because she has an opening, and I decided right there on the spot to do it.

The mind invents reasons afterward to explain the action. But the real truth is that such a "decision" isn't "made" at all. It happens. Suddenly, out of nowhere, the way appears. That's how I got to Springwater. And now, here I go, back to California.

I told everyone I was leaving, going back to California. In my imagination, I was already a Zen priest, my head shaved, wearing long black robes and carrying a stick of incense. I was going back to Anne North. In my imagination she had changed her mind, and we were lovers after all. I was going back to where there were queers and cripples and Communists and macrobiotics all over the place, back to a place where I "belonged," back to the ocean and the golden light. In my imagination, I was no longer restless, no longer seeking.

In future-fantasies there are never any mosquitoes, headaches, irritating people, or anxious thoughts about where to go next. There is settled presence, the absence of seeking and wanting. This is the real heart's desire. In daydreams of future happiness, like at the moment of getting a desired object, we are no longer seeking. We relax. For one moment, we are just here, without wanting anything. The real appeal of the desired object or of the imagined future is the absence of desire! But we mistake the *object* for the source of our happiness at that moment. So then we think, "Oh . . . I have to have whatever it is, so I can feel this way." Just let go of the objects. Just let go of the postponement.

When I get to Berkeley, *then* I'll let go. . . .

78

The September retreat was so light. White flowers from which the bees drink silence, their bellies against the velvet petals in the orange light of early morning, a ruby-throated hummingbird suspended before me. A tiny, tiny, almost microscopic red-orange spider transversing a white petal. There is the smell of skunk in the lower field, and one woman from New York City who was so busy and uptight when she arrived is lying now curled on the earth in the morning sun.

215

Passing from awareness to thoughts again and again without judgment, identification, or storyline. Just passing. Can waking up really be this simple?

There were two pregnant women at this retreat, so we had several unborn retreatants enjoying the quiet, and there was also a mother and her eight-year-old child. The family was staying nearby and the mother was attending the retreat while the father did childcare—they had several children. The eight-year-old felt very connected to the retreat and told her mother she wanted to come and sit with us, so this child sat with her mother in the sitting room on several occasions, and even went (by herself) to a meeting with Toni. They listened to the rain together, Toni said, and the little girl's eyes were huge with wonder. I bet Toni's were, too! An enlightened meeting, nothing in the way.

Sitting with that little person, I felt so touched. Children are so genuine at that age. Sitting in her presence I felt a great sense of responsibility. A responsibility for this earth, and for my life, rather than the restlessness and self-pity that has so often consumed me.

The first traces of autumn appearing. Blood-red gashes in the foliage. Morning frost. Fields turning brown, filled with wildflowers and thistles, some in bloom, others dry and brittle. Colors like a bruise are coming out everywhere, the rosy sky awash in the pond. The wood thrushes are gone for the winter. The deer are getting their dark winter coats. The milkweed pods are purple and bulging with seeds, ready to burst. Me and someone else sitting on the bench at twilight watching the hills and the clouds. Heather the cat comes and sits between us doing cat meditation.

Toni urged me to go deeply into listening itself. Just listen, she said. Don't try to hold on to the things heard or seen, but instantly allow the next perception. Don't stop to analyze, or go back over them, or try to figure them out or clarify them. Just go on. Listening, holding on to nothing. Allow listening itself to unfold without interference of any kind.

79

My last night at Springwater. The sun has just gone down. My room is emptied, my car is loaded and ready to go. I walk up to the north field to say good-bye. It is a dark, stormy evening. Huge black clouds are rolling in from the north, and dark red ones full of blood and winter. A crying animal somewhere in the woods. Wind in my face.

I feel suddenly overwhelmed with tremendous gratitude for these two years here. The love is what's important, the love I feel with everyone here, so apparent when all the ideas and images dissolve. My eyes fill with tears, like the clouds in the sky, because there is so much beauty, because so much of it is missed.

A stormy dawn the morning I leave, almost raining, the trees blowing, a deer and her tiny fawn loping through the field, crows playing on the riotous wind.

And then the open road. A truck stop in Pennsylvania. A tuna sandwich in Ohio. The new moon over the highway. Darkness. Red sky. Smell of manure.

80

A human being is essentially a spiritual eye.
The skin and bones fall away.
Whatever you really see, you are that.

RUMI

I went back to California. Anne North and I became dear friends, but not lovers. I worked on this book. I sat with Joko again, and with Mel. I did solitary retreats at a Vedanta monastery in Olema. I loved being in solitude completely by myself, with no schedule at all. No books, no talks, no teacher.

I sat with Toni when she came to California. She stayed at the house where I was living, and it was the first time I really felt that we met each other as friends, on some entirely new ground. That was a delightful discovery.

I did a retreat in the desert with Jean Klein, and several others with him in the Bay Area. I spent time in the Camaldolese hermitage in Big Sur. I listened to tapes of Gangaji, read Nisargadatta, and worked with Joko over the telephone. I traveled to New Mexico, imagining that I would live there. I drove back to California to sit with Toni again.

I so desperately want to *do* something and have some Big Experience and Get Somewhere: How am I doing? Is this it?

Is this "Awareness"? Is this "Consciousness"? Is this "Emptiness"? Is this *it*? No, there's a tension in my left shoulder blade that shouldn't be there. I shouldn't be thinking. I have to stop thinking. I have to experience the tension. Am I experiencing it? Am I "not-knowing" it? Is this *it*? No, I don't think so. I haven't gotten to the bottom of it yet. What should I do?

On and on and on the mind churns.

There's such social pressure on all of us to "be productive" and busy in the world. During this retreat with Toni in California I was out walking one morning. I came upon some red berries on a bush with dewdrops hanging from them. I stopped and was playing with the dewdrops, like a little kid. Suddenly along came another person, and I froze. I felt as though I'd been caught masturbating in the middle of the road. Should I stop? Should I keep playing with the dewdrops? It was so obvious, the programming is so strong that it's not okay to be playing! It's forbidden.

Toni offers permission to do nothing at all. To play with dewdrops.

I was looking more and more deeply at wanting. Wanting experiences. Wanting to Get Somewhere. Wanting final, permanent enlightenment. Wanting to know, to understand, to figure it all out, to get it. Wanting security. The fear of everything blowing away. Wanting to control, to manage my life, to hold on. Seeing the mind doing this on ever more subtle levels.

Toni says, "All of this experience-mongering, wanting enlightenment and so forth, is a form of resistance. In a flow without resistance you don't have to know how you're doing. It's alive. It's the airplane. The wind. You know, it's such a relief to realize that we don't have to be anything."

I began to wonder again about my dependency on Toni. I went into a meeting during retreat and brought it up. How would I feel if tomorrow Toni turned around and left us, saying that she was into something else now and that this whole thing had been a huge mistake? Would I be devastated?

"What's the whole thing?" Toni asks.

I laughed and laughed and laughed.

Because that's the problem. I've got a *huge* "Thing" in my mind that I'm dragging along, trying to maneuver, alternately fighting with or chasing after. This enormous dead object that talks, and it's nothing but thought!

"There can't just be nothing!" I said, laughing—but I was serious. It's too simple! I was quoting P'ei Hsiu in his dialogue with Huang Po that Toni reads to us at the end of retreats:

> Q: *What is the Way and how must it be followed?*
> A: *What sort of* thing *do you suppose the Way to be, that you should wish to* follow *it?*
> Q: *Should we not seek for anything at all?*
> A: *By conceding this, you would save yourself a lot of mental effort.*
> Q: *But in this way everything would be eliminated. There cannot just be nothing.*
> A: *Who called it nothing? Who told you to eliminate anything? Look at the void in front of your eyes. How can you produce it or eliminate it?*

In the meeting room later, feeling how I want something from Toni, from our meeting, some final and permanent insight that will set me free forever. Listening to the wanting and to an airplane passing overhead. The thought comes up, the airplane isn't enough.

"The airplane isn't enough," Toni says, "but the listening is. It can get so quiet."

The next morning, completely absorbed in the sky while walking briskly between two buildings, I walked right into a concrete post. I had a huge egg on my forehead all week. There was no separation between me and the sky, I told Toni, and then suddenly there was no separation between me and the post either.

It rained one afternoon and I was in the meeting room with Toni, with that huge egg on my forehead, and we were sitting there together in complete silence listening to the rain, and then the thoughts began to bubble up. I started asking Toni questions, hoping to get answers from her that would enlighten me so that I would turn into an enlightened being who could just be there listening to the rain. Pretty funny. Those thoughts that bubble up are thoughts: "I'm not enlightened yet," "There's something I need to get," "Maybe Toni can give it to me," "This can't be it." It's *all* just thought.

"You need to take a quantum leap," Toni said to me.

A quantum leap.

What is it?

This way is so simple. We so rarely really allow it. We do

maybe for ten minutes, and then thought begins inventing programs and practices and ideologies. People keep saying, Oh, this is Dzogchen, This is Advaita, This is Zen, This is Vipassana. But I wonder, is it? The more I go into it, the more I think what Toni is proposing is something plainer. If we drop *all* that baggage and start afresh, listening openly, without *any* ideas, then where are we? Toni's work is the most radical do-nothing-at-all I've yet encountered.

This does not mean sloth, inertia, never getting out of bed, or unrestrained indulgence in addictive patterns. In fact, all the above would be *something,* the result of thought and thought-constructed ideas of self. And *trying* to get rid of thought (or self) is just another thought process. Hence, the radical task of total no-thingness. How seeing happens without creating a program is a continuous experiment. It is moment to moment.

It is not something you finish doing. And in a certain sense it is definitely work (or practice). It requires diligence, precision, honesty, great passion, and interest. But exactly what this work really is becomes less definable all the time. It is a process of transparency, a shift in perspective, like suddenly seeing the third dimension in one of those Magic Eye paintings. It can't be forced, and what is revealed was always already there.

Although I still sit for an hour every morning and usually for several hours in the evening as well, I feel now that this is no more an act of meditation than any other moment of the day. All the questions that arise, if I trace them back, arise from thought. Thought conjures up imaginary problems and then tries to solve them. It is all a form of postponement. The truth is exactly now. Immediate. Simple.

"There's nothing to get to the bottom of," Toni said. "Just one bottomless moment."

81

It becomes more and more simple. You begin to know that just the fact that you're alive is prayer.

MAGGIE ROSS

I made plans to attend the June retreat in Springwater. Before I went, I expanded it to a six-month visit. When I got here, I rejoined staff. Felix was gone, new people had come. Toni no longer showed videos of Krishnamurti in her apartment; now there were open discussions. The place felt lighter, healthier. I became the receptionist. Seasons came and went.

As always, I imagined myself elsewhere, back at the Zen center as a priest, down in San Diego with Joko, off in the Berkshires with the Pioneer Valley Zen monks, in India with Papaji or Ramesh, in Hawaii with Gangaji, in Berkeley with a career. Finally, in the dead of winter, I announced that I was leaving. I had decided to move back to California and become a Zen priest. It's amazing how many times we can replay the same movie before we wear it out. And maybe in some cases we never completely wear it out. Perhaps it just gets more and more transparent.

People here were sad that I was leaving. I had the sudden realization that I matter here. This scares me. Responsibility scares me. I had a certain uneasy feeling that I was making a mistake. But I still liked the image of myself as a Zen priest.

Sharon's eyes filled with tears when I told her I was going. I didn't expect that. I've been so focused on how different I feel from everyone here, but suddenly I began to realize how much we actually have in common, something that may have become more important to me than shared political views or shared sexual orientation or common cultural history or the same sense of humor. I realize how much I *like* being around the people who come here and the people who live here, even those who seem very different from me. It occurs to me that maybe I don't really *need* to be surrounded by other lesbians and macrobiotic leftists anymore. Maybe there is something much subtler than all of that, which is being touched upon here at Springwater. Maybe it is that possibility that has brought me here. Maybe I don't really want to go.

"The reason most of us come here," Toni says, "is because we're hemmed in by resistances and fears and would like to find a way out, usually imagining a much more complicated way than just being with what's there. That seems too unexalted, unspectacular. Simply discovering—quietly, subtly, vulnerably—what's happening."

Just being here, alive. Fully alive. I don't have to *do* anything. It's so utterly simple. Everything is just happening.

That's it. And then thought rebels against that simplicity. Because if this is all there is to it, then the drama will be over. And if the drama is over, then what?

Working on this book, reading through all my old journals, the truth was right here in front of me to see. Even Mel was telling me to stay here. "How do I know which path to choose?" I ask him. "It's usually the one that's right in front of you, most obvious," he replies. "Our suffering," he says, "is believing there's a way out." That's exactly what I'm always looking for, a way out. "You have to let go of the paths not taken," Mel continues, "and really allow yourself to penetrate the one you've chosen."

It occurred to me that if I were asked to explain meditation to a group of people who knew nothing about it, it would be this work of open listening without restrictions that I would want to convey to them, not formal Zen practice. While I can see value in traditional Zen practice, it isn't the approach that most interests me or grabs me. *This* is what interests me. This is where my heart is. This is where I actually am. So why am I conjuring up this Zen-priest fantasy again?

The February retreat began and quickly the whole dream of going back to Zen began to crumble. On the third day, everything cleared and I knew beyond any doubt that I wasn't leaving Springwater. It was like waking up from a dream. I'm staying here, because this is where I am. I don't want to leave this place, or this open way of working, or Toni, or this community. There was a somatic shift. My body came back home, to listening.

I came here because this work is what matters most to me. Toni asked me once in a recent meeting if I was completely sure that there was nowhere to go. Obviously I'm not completely sure. So the best thing I can do is stay right here and find out what it is that I'm running away from or seeking.

I tend to keep my life in the courtship phase. I don't do this deliberately or willfully, of course, but I see it more clearly all the time. I'm always leaving or arriving, so I never have to become commonplace or dependable or fully face the way reality isn't what I want it to be. Because in my mind I always know I'm leaving soon, so it doesn't matter. I keep my options open. I'm always planning what's next. I don't penetrate to a certain depth as a result. I am unfaithful to my actual life, or to life itself.

Nixon died, the man who ordered the dropping of more bombs than any other head of state in the history of the world. If there was one single man who symbolized everything I fought against in my youth, it was Richard Nixon. (Why change dicks in the middle of a screw, vote for Nixon in '72.) Oddly enough, I feel sad. We are intimately connected to our so-called enemies.

In Chicago, Uncle Harold had a leg amputated. Then he fell, put out an eye, and broke a collarbone. "I've fallen out of the world," he said to me on the phone, the words slurred from medication and strokes. "I don't know who I am, or where I am, or what I'm supposed to do." His mind slipping away.

Crying in a staff meeting, realizing how I've been waiting all my life for something big to happen around the bend, and I'm realizing that nothing is ever going to happen except this moment. What if I *really am* nobody?

Sitting up by the pond afterward at twilight. Some animal dying, being eaten, in the woods. Lots of crying and scuffling sounds and then silence. Lightning bugs and the moon in the sky. Some immeasurable grief. All my illusions emptying out.

I began listening to more tapes of Gangaji. She's a woman about my age, a former acupuncturist from California who went to India and had an awakening with Papaji, a guru in the Advaita Hindu tradition. Gangaji is a brilliant, sexy, charismatic woman who radiates love, and sees with breathtaking acuity. She has tremendous confidence and intuitive spontaneity. Something about her has made me feel cautious in the past, something that seems seductive, inflated, mesmerizing, dangerous in some way. Sometimes I think that people around her are giving too many blissed-out testimonials. I don't trust it.

But nevertheless I began listening to her again, and her tapes had a powerful impact on me this time. Gangaji cuts through people's stories without a moment's hesitation, usually before they get one sentence out. "Don't touch the story," she says emphatically. Stop your addictions, just stop. She talks about the willingness to directly experience whatever is arising, without repressing or discharging it, without denying or acting it out, without analyzing or sentimentalizing it or telling a story about it. Gangaji adamantly refuses all postponements, and points you directly back to the source. Stop the search, she says. Truth is not some imagined state that hasn't arrived yet.

I felt as though I were in love. I went around the house singing. I put her picture up in my room. The side of Gangaji that had frightened me became attractive, her unabashed enjoyment of devotional love, her ebullient sense of fun, the effortless ease of her approach, her boldness. If this is a seduction, why am I resisting it? Am I afraid of losing control, losing face, losing my mind, losing my friends? I am so tired of holding back. Gangaji calls it the disease of sophistication, this wanting to appear unaffected, this fear of adoration or of speaking the truth too strongly. Don't hold back, she urges, don't be restrained. Drop the disclaimers, the "yes, buts." Her encouragement of devotional ecstasy and unequivocal truth-speaking touches a profound yearning in me.

"I'm in love," a woman told Gangaji on one tape I heard, meaning in love with Gangaji.

I cringed. Oh my God. I could imagine what Toni would do with *that*. It made me very uncomfortable. I *felt* in love with Gangaji, but I would *never* say it to her, certainly not out loud in public! I was keeping my love for her in the closet. It was something I found slightly embarrassing and even shameful. I "knew" it was a dangerous delusion.

To my utter surprise, Gangaji responded to this woman by saying something like, "What a beautiful declaration!" As if she had just heard something truly delightful. And then she said, "Now just drop the *in*."

I *am* love. Gangaji accepted the woman's love, celebrated it, and pointed it back to its true source. There is something about this that I find enormously healing, an antidote to my Protestant-puritan streak that is always so serious, trying so hard. Gangaji has some quality of heart-warmth and willingness to allow ecstasy and love and divine in-loveness to exist, not just "allow them to exist," but actually take them out of the closet and celebrate them, enjoy them, fall into them completely. Be in love. Naked, foolish, willing to go over the edge. Probably this is dangerous, but it's also vitalizing. Listening to Gangaji's satsangs, I was touched on many levels of being, and something began to unfold within me.

I stopped biting my fingers. Gangaji said just stop these old habits, don't pick them up, surrender everything, and I did. I *knew* I would never pick it up again, the way I know I won't start drinking or smoking again. I've *never* felt that about biting before, completely certain that I was done with it. The whole thing just lost its power and fell away. It was as if a switch had been flipped in my mind. I *saw* that I don't have to continue it. It wasn't an effort of willpower to stop, but more like a surrender or relaxation, giving up the practice (or effort) of biting, giving up the *idea* that I am addicted. The *thought* that was always there before that "this habit is really big and old and out of control and insurmountable and I won't be able to stop," that thought was suddenly transparent and powerless. The whole thing unraveled and was gone.

I began imagining myself running off to Hawaii to be with Gangaji. I would leave Springwater and move to Maui. Or maybe I would go to India to meet Papaji, her guru, the source of it all. Finally I booked a plane flight to California in July so I could see Gangaji there.

❀

And then my mother fell on the bus and broke her hip and I was leaving suddenly, unexpectedly, for Chicago, my trip to California to see Gangaji canceled. I spent the summer in hospitals and rehabilitation centers. It was precious to have that close time with my mother, and I also sat with a lot of feelings about death, impermanence, vulnerability—seeing my mother in pain, watching her learn to walk again. My fears about money and being nobody bubbled up, and I started worrying about needing a career. Just before I left Chicago, I started to bite my fingers again.

It was late summer when I returned to Springwater, and the moon was full. So many dreams had dried up. My enormous breakthrough with my finger-biting addiction had apparently gone up in smoke, my decision to stay at Springwater was on shaky ground again, I was confused, and it all felt very old and familiar and stuck.

I could hear Toni and Joko and Gangaji all telling me in their different voices to directly experience confusion, and the desire to bite, and the anger or fear underneath that—to experience them as pure, sensate perception, without the story. To listen to the thoughts and see them as thoughts. And if biting happens, and *seems* uncontrollable, then experience biting. Totally. Feel the sensations. Hear the thoughts.

But instead I fall into a mental haze, thinking of other things, or thinking *about* what's happening, identifying it as "my" confusion, "my" addiction. I told Toni that I was in despair because I *saw* these habits, future-thinking and finger-biting, but they just kept coming back. Year after year after year after year.

"Here's where you have to be really discerning," Toni replied. "When you say that you *see* them, is it really seeing, or is it *thinking?* Thinking about how long they've persisted, how it's never going to end, how it's hopeless, wanting to know how to fix it. That isn't seeing. That's thinking."

This work (or life itself) is so simple! Yet we resist and resist it. We keep looking for imaginary solutions.

❦

I called Joko and told her I was having thoughts of moving to San Diego so I could work more closely with her.

"I think you should stay right where you are," Joko replied.

Joko is doing what she calls systems work lately. As I understand it, a system is any habitual, conditioned pattern of behavior by which we go away from being here. Joko suggests working with systems by observing them, identifying them, and then deliberately going against them. Not because doing this will make you a better person, but in order to bring up the terror that underlies the system, so you can experience it. Fully experiencing that terror in the body, nonverbally, is the gate to awakening. It's basically the same thing Gangaji and Toni also talk about, the willingness to directly experience what's there as sensation, without naming it or telling ourselves a story about it (what it is and how it got there and how long it will probably last and how hopeless it is), but just being still and feeling it out all the way to the bottom, where it is revealed to be nothing at all.

So I was telling Joko that obviously one of my major systems is thinking about the future, always imagining myself elsewhere, and actually going from one place to another. So she asks me how I could go against that system.

"Well, I guess I could make a commitment to stay here at Springwater for some period of time."

Joko agrees. She advises me not to make it too grandiose. Don't promise to stay for the next twenty years. It has to be doable, but on the other hand, it must be long enough to bring up the terror.

Two years popped into my head immediately.

I spent the next several weeks trying to chisel it down to one year, but that didn't seem to bring up any terror. Two years definitely did. Finally I took the plunge and told everyone I knew that I was making a two-year commitment to stay here.

I went through a few weeks of sheer hell. Every waking moment was consumed in thoughts of where I wanted to go, and trying to figure out how I could get out of this commitment without losing face, and feeling horrible.

But then something shifted. I woke up. I looked around, and discovered this is really a very nice life I have here. I stopped thinking about the future.

82

"Joan, I think you should stop reading all those spiritual books," Roger said to me. "I used to sit all the time when I first got here," he told me, "hours and hours every day. And then I realized I was just trying to have some big experience. And so I stopped. I think you're trying too hard." Roger's eyes were radiant. And then he belched.

Joko says, Enlightenment is final defeat, not final victory.

Staying here is about giving up hope, realizing that this is it. I feel settled in a way I never have before, appreciative of my actual life. The men on staff have become like brothers to me. So different we are, yet so intimate. The tenderness with which we live and work together is quite touching. All the identities I've clung to seem to be melting away.

Toni told a joke during retreat about a man who thought he was a wheat kernel. He was put in a mental hospital, and after a while the psychiatrist felt he was cured and the man was released. On his way home the man saw a chicken crossing the road and he ran back to the mental hospital in terror. "I thought it was clear to you now that you're not a wheat kernel," the psychiatrist says to the man. "It's clear to me," the man replies, "but I wasn't sure it would be clear to the chicken."

I walk through the field to the garden on Thanksgiving morning, unlatch the gate, brush snow from the kale plants, pick the green leaves. A single chickadee sings. We are mostly water and space, Toni says. Water and space.

The full moon rises like paper over the wintry landscape, a red disk that grows smaller, brighter, more substantial as it climbs into the sky. Deer graze in the moonlight beneath planets and stars, and I am struck by the way it all holds together. At dawn the sky is red. There is a wild, fierce wind, and the crows are flying sideways, blown across the sky.

How much possibility there is. The limits are only imagined. Freedom is seeing, effortlessly, that thought does not have to be followed. Everything is happening. We're not in control. And we're not out of control either, because there is no "me" separate from the totality to manage it or be overrun by it. When we don't know anything, then anything is possible. The conditioned patterns can drop completely, because they are imaginary. This capacity to step out of the story is the "choice" my therapist Sophie offered me when I sobered up, it is the freedom that all true spiritual teachers transmit, it is what I saw and loved in Malcolm X years ago.

I don't *have* to keep picking up the old images, the habits, the belief that something is missing. It is possible to be quiet, listen, and discover what is. In that discovery, habits lose their power. If they pop up, they can be seen nonjudgmentally, with affectionate curiosity and interest.

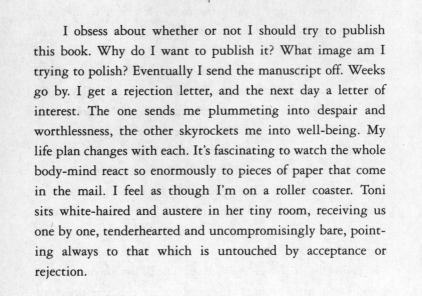

I obsess about whether or not I should try to publish this book. Why do I want to publish it? What image am I trying to polish? Eventually I send the manuscript off. Weeks go by. I get a rejection letter, and the next day a letter of interest. The one sends me plummeting into despair and worthlessness, the other skyrockets me into well-being. My life plan changes with each. It's fascinating to watch the whole body-mind react so enormously to pieces of paper that come in the mail. I feel as though I'm on a roller coaster. Toni sits white-haired and austere in her tiny room, receiving us one by one, tenderhearted and uncompromisingly bare, pointing always to that which is untouched by acceptance or rejection.

Spring is coming again. The deer with a broken leg has survived the winter, I saw her in the lower field last night. A chipmunk who has woken up from hibernation is singing his heart out in the morning, standing upright on the stone ledge amidst the first crocuses. An insect crawls into my ear.

The ambiguity about whether or not to publish the book has vanished. Now I believe in the project completely. Something ignited in response to interest and possibility, some energy and conviction, like a flower blooming. I realized I *do* care about this book, but because of what it has to say. The other part is there too, promoting *myself,* but it isn't the whole story. Maybe the truth about human life is that it endlessly reveals a mosaic of motives if we are willing to see them, and nothing is perfect or immaculate if measured against our ideals of how we think we ought to be. We have no idea, really, why we're writing a book or trying to get it published, or why we're living at a retreat center. It's happening.

Weeks go by and I wait to hear the verdict from several publishers who are interested, doing everything I can now to advance the project. I am praying, lighting candles, sending off faxes. Holding my breath. And then one day, miraculously, the prayer is answered.

Everything changes in an instant. Nobody from nowhere becomes somebody. I am ecstatic. My mother is overjoyed. My friends are elated. Uncle Harold says I finally have authority to speak. How seductive, what a rush, how genuinely enjoyable, and how fickle and fragile. It's all meaningless on one level, image-bubbles with no substance whatsoever. Nothing has really changed at all. And in another sense something *has* changed. Like having a partner in a dance, getting published changes the whole gestalt. There is a potential for interaction and exchange that is new, a commerce. I am entering the world in a new way.

I imagine the cover of my book with my name on it, the thrill of that. I imagine it without my name, anonymous, and discover I am less enthusiastic. Can all this be seen with interest, without the urge to correct myself, which is only more of the same self-centered movement?

I feel the pressure of "success," pressure to keep it up, to sell enough books, to write more books, to uphold some new and better image, to be the Joan Tollifson my readers will expect, which is certainly a more enlightened person than who I really am. I try to be more enlightened. Instead, I find myself growing irritated and explosive, shouting at someone on staff, being almost belligerent with Toni. If anything, I seem to be worsening by the minute. I tell Toni that my next book will have to be called *The Fool I Still Am.*

Roger comes to my room, brings me a peach from the tree in the garden.

I am suddenly terrified of the exposure of my life to the public, the potential for being misunderstood, my worst nightmare. I call Joko.

"You have a requirement that people understand you," Joko says. "But the truth is what?"

"Sometimes they do, sometimes they don't."

"Right. Your practice is to experience what it is when they don't."

I was comfortable with failure, but success is unfamiliar. A whole new set of tapes is playing, a whole new set of challenges, and the possibility for greater humiliations. I recall a passage in a book by Hubert Benoit that struck me very strongly when I read it. Benoit says that all negative states are at bottom humiliations, and that humiliation is the gateway to awakening.

Humiliation, he says, comes from trying not to see our powerlessness, holding on to the picture of a "me" who is separate from the totality, striving to triumph in some way. Benoit maintains that the true guru is "reality as it is, our daily life," which inevitably defeats our ambitions and reveals our lack of control. Even the most successful book eventually turns to dust, and its author as well; and along the way that author will invariably meet many people who feel that the book was a waste of paper, that the author was an ass. Benoit points out that our deliberate spiritual "doings" tend to prevent awakening because they all aim, directly or indirectly, at "on high," whereas awakening awaits us "beneath," in finally, fully experiencing the bottom-line defeat that we have been running from so frantically. This absolute defeat is the end of all imagined limitation and bondage, of all imaginary salvation, and of all imagining that there is someone to save.

It is of the utmost importance to realize that humility is not a facade to be worn or a method to be practiced. "If I don't understand that," Benoit says, "I shall avoid humiliations instead of using them." Merely to abstain from all situations that may involve ego-aggrandizement or pride is nothing more than an attempt to cultivate a false humility that is actually about safety and image, and has nothing whatsoever to do with true emptiness. True humility comes from jumping into the fire, and fully experiencing the conflagration that life offers. Awakening is giving up all hope of improvement, all need of something better. It is fully present, immediate being, with no escape from exactly what is. Not as a method with an imagined result, but as a possibility, moment to moment.

We search for gurus, for ideal states, for enlightenment, a better life, a more perfect self. We analyze, we think, we strain to finally, totally "get it," to know the answer, to do the right thing. And in the end—in sleep, or death, or waking up—it all dissolves into silence.

I remember an afternoon at the rehabilitation-nursing facility where my mother was last summer after she broke her hip. I stepped for a moment into the chapel, where a white-haired woman sat alone in her wheelchair, singing. I listened, unseen, at the doorway. The old woman sang with ardor, her voice untainted by the events of a lifetime, her song continuing on this page. Who writes these words, or any words?

In the woods, I find a heap of torn feathers in the leaves, from something that was ravaged in the night, devoured, consumed. In Chicago, Uncle Harold dies, a week before his ninetieth birthday.

A praying mantis delicately finds her way up the side of the building. In the woods, the inchworms descend on invisible threads. A grasshopper has died atop a blooming Queen Anne's lace. There is a rustling sound in the air, the rattle of death from the north. Clouds pass through me, dark green, leaves turning colors again and blowing off the trees.

Life becomes simpler and simpler, ordinary things more

precious: small talk in the kitchen, the tick of the clock, a hug in the morning from Roger, the fire-red cardinal who lands for an instant in the green grass, a cup of tea with Sharon. The upsets get more interesting and less upsetting. Sometimes I even welcome them.

Other Bell Tower Books

*Books that nourish the soul, illuminate the mind,
and speak directly to the heart*

Valeria Alfeyeva
PILGRIMAGE TO DZHVARI
*A Woman's Journey
of Spiritual Awakening*
An unforgettable introduction to
the riches of the Eastern Orthodox
mystical tradition. A modern *Way
of a Pilgrim.*
0–517–88389–9 Softcover

Tracy Cochran and Jeff Zaleski
TRANSFORMATIONS
*Awakening to the Sacred in
Ourselves*
An exploration of enlightenment
experiences and the ways in which
they can transform our lives.
0–517–70150–2 Hardcover

David A. Cooper
**ENTERING THE SACRED
MOUNTAIN**
*Exploring the Mystical Practices
of Judaism, Buddhism,
and Sufism*
An inspiring chronicle of one
man's search for truth.
0–517–88464–X Softcover

David A. Cooper
THE HEART OF STILLNESS
*The Elements of
Spiritual Practice*
A comprehensive guidebook to
the principles of inner work.
0–517–88187–X Softcover

David A. Cooper
**SILENCE, SIMPLICITY, AND
SOLITUDE**
A Guide for Spiritual Retreat
Required reading for anyone
contemplating a retreat.
0–517–88186–1 Softcover

Marc David
NOURISHING WISDOM
*A Mind/Body Approach to
Nutrition and Well-Being*
A book that advocates awareness
in eating.
0–517–88129–2 Softcover

Kat Duff
THE ALCHEMY OF ILLNESS
A luminous inquiry into the
function and purpose of illness.
0–517–88097–0 Softcover

Noela N. Evans
**MEDITATIONS FOR
THE PASSAGES
AND CELEBRATIONS
OF LIFE**
A Book of Vigils
Articulating the often unspoken
emotions experienced at such
times as birth, death, and
marriage.
0–517–59341–6 Hardcover
0–517–88299–X Softcover

Bernard Glassman &
Rick Fields
**INSTRUCTIONS TO
THE COOK**
*A Zen Master's Lessons in Living
a Life that Matters*
A distillation of Zen wisdom that
can be used equally well as a
manual on business or spiritual
practice, cooking, or life.
0–517–70377–7 Hardcover

Burghild Nina Holzer
A WALK BETWEEN HEAVEN AND EARTH
A Personal Journal on Writing and the Creative Process
How keeping a journal focuses and expands our awareness of ourselves and everything that touches our lives.
0–517–88096–2 *Softcover*

Greg Johanson and Ron Kurtz
GRACE UNFOLDING
Psychotherapy in the Spirit of the Tao-te ching
The interaction of client and therapist illuminated through the gentle power and wisdom of Lao Tsu's ancient classic.
0–517–88130–6 *Softcover*

Selected by
Marcia and Jack Kelly
ONE HUNDRED GRACES
Mealtime Blessings
A collection of graces from many traditions, inscribed in calligraphy reminiscent of the manuscripts of medieval Europe.
0–517–58567–7 *Hardcover*
0–517–88230–2 *Softcover*

Jack and Marcia Kelly
SANCTUARIES
A Guide to Lodgings in Monasteries, Abbeys, and Retreats of the United States
For those in search of renewal and a little peace; described by the *New York Times* as "the *Michelin Guide* of the retreat set."
THE NORTHEAST
0–517–57727–5 *Softcover*
THE WEST COAST & SOUTHWEST
0–517–88007–5 *Softcover*

THE COMPLETE U.S.
0–517–88517–4 *Softcover*

Marcia M. Kelly
HEAVENLY FEASTS
Memorable Meals in Monasteries, Abbeys, and Retreats
Delectable repasts savored by the Kellys on their monastic travels.
0–517–88522–0 *Softcover*

Barbara Lachman
THE JOURNAL OF HILDEGARD OF BINGEN
A year in the life of the twelfth-century German saint— the diary she never had the time to write herself.
0–517–59169–3 *Hardcover*
0–517–88390–2 *Softcover*

Katharine Le Mée
CHANT
The Origins, Form, Practice, and Healing Power of Gregorian Chant
The ways in which this ancient liturgy can nourish us and transform our lives.
0–517–70037–9 *Hardcover*

Gunilla Norris
BECOMING BREAD
Meditations on Loving and Transformation
A book linking the food of the spirit—love—with the food of the body—bread.
0–517–59168–5 *Hardcover*

Gunilla Norris
BEING HOME
A Book of Meditations
An exquisite modern book of
hours, a celebration of
mindfulness in everyday activities.
0–517–58159–0 *Hardcover*

Gunilla Norris
JOURNEYING IN PLACE
*Reflections from
a Country Garden*
Another classic book of
meditations illuminating the
sacredness of daily experience.
0–517–59762–4 *Hardcover*

Gunilla Norris
SHARING SILENCE
*Meditation Practice and
Mindful Living*
A book describing the essential
conditions for meditating in a
group or on one's own.
0–517–59506–0 *Hardcover*

Ram Dass and Mirabai Bush
COMPASSION IN ACTION
*Setting Out
on the Path of Service*
Heartfelt encouragement and
advice for those ready to commit
time and energy to relieving
suffering in the world.
0–517–88500-X *Softcover*

His Holiness
Shantanand Saraswati
**THE MAN WHO WANTED
TO MEET GOD**
*Myths and Stories that Explain
the Inexplicable*
The teaching stories of one of
India's greatest living saints.
0–517–88520–4 *Softcover*

Rabbi Rami M. Shapiro
**WISDOM OF
THE JEWISH SAGES**
A Modern Reading of Pirke Avot
A third-century treasury of
maxims on justice, integrity, and
virtue—Judaism's principal
ethical scripture.
0–517–79966–9 *Hardcover*

Ed. Richard Whelan
SELF-RELIANCE
*The Wisdom of Ralph Waldo
Emerson as Inspiration for
Daily Living*
A distillation of Emerson's
spiritual writings for
contemporary readers.
0–517–58512-X *Softcover*

*Bell Tower books are for sale at your local bookstore or you may call
Random House at 1-800-793-BOOK to order with a credit card.*